A Guide to
Teaching Practice in Ireland

A Guide to
Teaching Practice in Ireland

Brendan Walsh and Rose Dolan

Gill & Macmillan

Gill & Macmillan Ltd
Hume Avenue
Park West
Dublin 12
with associated companies throughout the world
www.gillmacmillan.ie

978 07171 45119

Index compiled by Cover to Cover
Print origination in Ireland by TypeIT, Dublin

The paper used in this book is made from the wood pulp of managed forests.
For every tree felled, at least one tree is planted, thereby renewing natural resources.

Contents

Foreword

When does a teacher cease being a student-teacher? In the context of a changing world, it is increasingly clear that teachers must continuously respond, adapt and refine to remain relevant and authoritative in the classroom environment.

For those teachers in Ireland now reaching the end of their careers, the extent and challenge of this changing world is probably most apparent in the area of technology. Regardless of economic upheavals of boom or bust, the proliferation and democratisation of computer technology, mobile telephony and the World Wide Web are all irreversible. These are all phenomena of the past three decades. They have emerged in the course of the working lives of this generation of teachers. Those teachers who for whatever reason have failed to keep abreast of these developments or to explore their potential application in the classroom are now far adrift of the world in which schoolchildren live.

This teaching generation has also been confronted with many other challenges which, while perhaps less tangible or visible as those of technology, are not any the less significant. These include changing cultural patterns; changing social structures in areas such as family and community; a changing understanding of the nature of learning and changing expectations of schooling itself. All of these impact in different and complex ways on the life and role of the teacher. No teacher can take refuge in denial.

And so, to the extent that a Guide typically navigates a route from a starting position to a predefined and identified destination, this one is rather different. It is so because teacher development is a process of ongoing renewal and becoming rather than one of departure and arrival.

This Guide, therefore, provides the student-teacher with the essential underpinning tools and strategies which can enable such a process to unfold. It does this by being relentlessly true to the reality of the Irish classroom today and to the actuality of the challenges and stresses by which teachers are daily confronted. It shows that it is by acknowledging and recognising one's anxieties and vulnerabilities that the student-teacher is laying down the foundation for self-awareness and reflexivity.

Teacher development, however, is more than a process of reactive, reflective contemplation. As our understanding of the process of learning grows, teachers themselves are leading a dialogue, inside the profession and outside it, on the nature of the role and its associated competences. Of particular significance here is the move away from teaching as a process of 'imparting knowledge' towards teaching as a process of enabling discovery and exploration. This changing emphasis has major implications for the art and craft of teaching. It impacts on the nature of the relationship between the teacher and the students; on the relationships between the students themselves; on issues such as class planning, classroom management and discipline; and on the wider school climate. It is also manifest in the manner in which children with special education needs are included in, and impact upon, the pedagogical culture of the school.

Teaching and schooling of course are never entirely self-contained. They operate within wider overarching policy frameworks which carry increasing demands of scrutiny and accountability. While such demands are of a multiple nature, the approach to assessment as implemented through the state examination system is probably the most important and pervasive factor.

The pressing demands of the two terminal state examinations in Irish second level schools, the Junior Certificate and the Leaving Certificate, are a constant backdrop to the discussion on teacher effectiveness, teacher development and pedagogical innovation. The task of navigating the tension between the demands of a summative assessment process on the one hand and those of a formative approach on the other is an ever present one in Irish second level classrooms. This Guide makes a significant contribution to our thinking as to how to manage this contested space.

It makes clear also, however, that the ultimate challenge for every teacher is to define and create his or her own unique individual persona as a teacher in that special interplay between the teacher, the students and the subject matter.

Professor Tom Collins
Professor of Education and Dean of Teaching and Learning NUI Maynooth

Introduction

We shall not cease from exploration
And the end of all our exploring
Will be to arrive where we started
And know the place for the first time.

T. S. ELIOT, *The Four Quartets*

If you're beginning to teach in the second level system in Ireland, or are a recently qualified teacher, this is the book for you; a comprehensive, accessible and practice-based text that you can consult when you have questions about teaching. These might relate to developing your classroom practice, understanding the system that you are working in or deepening your awareness of the needs of your pupils. Whatever these questions are, you'll find answers, direction and signposts to further information between the covers of this guide to teaching practice.

Education in Ireland has changed radically since the early to mid-1990s and, while general teaching methods are shared by teachers throughout the world, the specific changes now occurring in Irish schools mean that you, our aspiring teachers, require a text tailored to meet your specific needs. It is our hope that it will prove an invaluable guide and source of encouragement.

Teaching is a demanding profession, yet we can think of no more fulfilling career. The early years are both challenging and rewarding, leading to the emergence of the teacher you want to become and finally to embracing teaching and learning as a way of living, which involves working within a dedicated learning community with its own culture, history and professional vernacular.

The art of teaching is not black and white but rather comprises the shades of grey between. As we learn to teach, we come to understand what we do and why we do it, we learn to think on our feet in the classroom in response to the emerging learning that is the heart of the endeavour, to decide what is pedagogically suitable in a given moment by drawing on deep skills and comprehensive knowledge, to initiate others into the human story, the conversation of humankind.

This wider understanding is always at the peril of being lost in discussions concerning measurability, testing, 'relevance' and so forth, but be assured that the personal, human interaction of teaching, the joy of seeing young people engage with a worthwhile body of knowledge, remains at the heart of teaching. With this in mind, we offer this text as advice and guidance. It is informed by the belief that, ultimately, teaching is about helping children to learn, and in facilitating that process, we enter into a profoundly rewarding and worthwhile personal engagement both with our pupils and with our discipline.

We wrote this book based on the insight and expertise gained from a combined experience of twenty years of post-primary teaching, our involvement in scholarship concerning initial teacher education and the needs of newly qualified teachers in Ireland, and the knowledge and expertise we bring to bear in our work as Course Leader/Director of Initial Teacher Education programmes at two Irish universities.

The book is divided into three sections. Section One describes the development, culture and present state of the Irish education system. It details how the system assumed its present shape and how the various types of institutions (e.g. vocational, comprehensive, etc.) came into being, and provides a detailed overview of the most recent developments in practice and policy. The second part of Section One offers advice on what you, the prospective student-teacher, should consider before embarking upon initial teacher education.

Section Two deals with the practice of teaching and learning and provides comprehensive and detailed guidance regarding, for example, preparation for teaching, designing lesson plans, the key features of good classroom teaching and evaluation of one's own teaching and of pupil learning. This section also provides practical, realistic and practice-based advice on dealing with pupil behaviour and classroom management. The challenges and rewards of working with children with special education needs are also addressed.

Section Three deals with your development as a teacher, through engagement in critical reflection about teaching and learning, learning from your teaching practice placement and its supervision, and providing you with advice on all aspects of these processes. Supervision sometimes causes unnecessary concern to student-teachers and this section provides advice on engaging with it in a constructive, sensible manner, leading to better teaching and enhanced learning. Finally, this section provides an overview of what the newly qualified teacher needs to consider in his/her first year of professional teaching. Along with practical suggestions regarding time management, evaluation (homework, etc.), working with parents and overcoming initial difficulties, it also encourages you to reflect upon your own professional development as a teacher in order to help you to become the teacher you want to become.

We hope you find this book useful and informative and wish you every success with your initial teacher education studies!

Brendan Walsh and Rose Dolan

SECTION ONE
– THE SCHOOL SYSTEM

1

The Irish Education System: Practice and Process

Brendan Walsh

INTRODUCTION

This chapter explains the development, operation and contemporary status of post-primary schooling in Ireland. The authors assume that the aspiring teacher, wishing as s/he does to become part of the teaching community, is anxious to understand the historical and sociological evolution of that community. Teaching is an ancient profession and has profound historical antecedents. Becoming a teacher is not simply about amassing a set of 'skills' or 'methods' that will somehow, magically, enable someone to operate 'effectively' in a classroom.

There is wide-ranging scholarly discussion concerning what, exactly, the decision to teach entails. Is it, for example, a commitment to a way of living? A commitment to the promulgation of one's discipline? A desire to work with and see adolescents flourish as moral and civically minded individuals? The decision to teach entails entering into a community of practitioners as old as humankind. Just as the practice of teaching has developed over millennia, so too have systems and structures of education. It is significant that some contemporary elements of teaching and schooling differ little from those of ancient Rome, or medieval Europe; this is because teaching is a profoundly human activity.

Instruction to the young is part of the DNA of humankind; it is, as Michael Oakeshott reflected, an initiation into the conversation between the generations. It is, ultimately, about learning how to become human within the human family.

Deciding to teach, therefore, entails entering into a system that has evolved over many centuries. In Ireland, for example, our history as a colonial territory and the emphasis of Irish educational history over the past two decades has tended to underemphasise the culture of learning that existed in Ireland prior to the establishment of the National Education System in 1831. This is also partly due to the enormous quantity of data generated after this date. Leaving aside such debates, it is important for the aspiring teacher to realise that s/he is entering into a complex system that has evolved and developed in the way it has because of specific pressures, needs and influences.

In Ireland, this has produced three categories of post-primary school, each with its own ethos and mission. These schools differ for particular historic, social and economic reasons. Also, within these categories, schools differ widely in their individual culture and manner of operating. Importantly, schooling, and to a lesser extent teaching, has been the subject of intense scrutiny over the past twenty-five years, resulting in significant changes during the 1990s.

Within a very short time span, the operation of schools and their wider role have become the subject of extensive public and political interest. Post-primary schools are now open to regular evaluation (information that is made publicly available), their workings are expected to be open and transparent, and they are encouraged to take on an ever-increasing role in repairing social fracture and disengagement.

It is important, therefore, that the aspiring teacher gains a sound understanding of the complexity, diversity, function and aspirations of the education system they are choosing to work within. Teaching is becoming a less isolated practice and in choosing to teach, with all the extraordinary possibilities and rewards that it promises, we choose to become part of a system and tradition possessed of its own culture, vernacular, methodologies, antecedents and history.

The following helps to provide a contextual overview of this evolution, explaining how and why schooling has developed the way it has in Ireland and provides an up-to-date outline of requirements and regulations for those thinking about entering the profession.

THE EVOLUTION OF POST-PRIMARY INSTITUTIONS IN IRELAND

Maintaining the Status Quo: 1922–57

Before the advent of independence in 1922, the British authorities administered Ireland's education system. Having weathered the storms of denominational controversy in the nineteenth century, it came under the scrutiny of nationalists in the early years of the twentieth century. Patrick Pearse, the schoolteacher and leader of the Dublin Rising of 1916, famously denounced the Intermediate (post-primary) system as a grinding 'murder machine'.

With the advent of independence, post-primary schools in particular were left to continue under the largely denominational structure that had developed during the nineteenth century. They operated independently and government involvement was minimal. The Commission for Intermediate Education (1921) insisted that its programme for secondary schools was 'merely helpful and suggestive' and encouraged schools to draw up their own programmes. The newly independent state was explicit concerning its relationship with post-primary schools: 'The state ... neither founds secondary schools, nor finances ... nor appoints teachers ... nor exercises any power or veto over ... appointments(s) or dismissal of ... teachers or the management of schools.'

The curriculum of secondary schools remained of the classical type and catered for a very small percentage of the population. In 1925, for example, fewer than 1,000 pupils sat the Leaving Certificate examination. The curriculum seemed irrelevant and, in 1926, the Commission on Technical Education drew up a list of proposals later contained in the Vocational Education Act (1930). The act reflected the growing realisation that schooling in Ireland failed to attract those who could not benefit from an academic curriculum and was informed by the principles of economic imperative.

This was the origin of the Vocational Education System. It was the first state-sponsored system of schooling after independence and marked a definite movement away from the traditional model of Church-owned and managed schools. This, however, did not mean that government was prepared to become involved in wholesale provision of post-primary schooling. Minister for Education Richard Mulcahy (1948–51 and 1954–7) described his role as a 'very, very narrow one'. Mulcahy instigated the Council of Education (1950) to inquire into the primary and secondary curriculum. The council reported that there was no reason to make significant changes and described calls for greater access to secondary schooling as 'utopian' and economically unrealistic. Mulcahy's successor, Seán Moylan, was equally dismissive of greater access, rejecting the 'idea of equal opportunities for all'. Mulcahy became Minister for Education for a second time between 1954 and 1957, but the period witnessed no radical change in curricular content, access or provision.

The period between 1922 and 1957, then, was not characterised by innovation or experimentation. It was widely accepted that secondary schooling was the preserve of the middle class, most effectively managed by private or religious bodies. Innovation and access were limited by economic considerations and meaningful pedagogical considerations were strikingly absent.

Changing Times: 1957–84

Fianna Fáil won the general election of 1957 and remained in power for sixteen years. Seán Lemass replaced Eamon de Valera as Taoiseach in 1959 on the cusp of the radical changes that characterised the 1960s. While post-primary enrolment had grown from under 12,000 in 1925 to almost 24,000 in 1959, people such as Noël Browne argued that the system reinforced social hierarchies: '... labourers continue to be labourers, and the doctors can make their sons doctors, lawyers, architects and so on.' In 1959, a comparative list of expenditure on education revealed that Russia was spending £7 per head, America £5 and England £2, while Ireland was spending approximately ten shillings.

The early 1960s witnessed a growing awareness of the very limited nature of secondary school provision; post-primary schooling remained, in effect, the concern of the few. In 1963, the Labour Party published *Challenge and Change in Education*, a policy document calling for free education. Minister for Education Dr Patrick Hillery (1959–65) responded by committing the government to providing increased educational opportunities for all, and to the establishment of regional technical colleges (RTCs) and comprehensive schools. These were designed to provide for non-academic pupils not catered for in traditional secondary schools and reflected the government's growing awareness of the relationship between economic welfare and technical education.

This link was emphasised by the *Investment in Education Report* (1965). It was critical of: the high level of early school leavers; the low rate of participation in secondary level and university by 'many social groups'; 'inequalities in participation in post-primary education ... based on social group and geographical location'; and pointed to 'significant disparities' in 'participation in the educational sector among various socio-economic and regional groups'. The report presented a bleak picture of underinvestment and underachievement.

The relationship between provision and social fairness was reflected in the opposition party's 1966 document *Fine Gael for a Just Society*, which criticised the government for not grasping the 'many nettles' involved in social policy. Unexpectedly, in 1967, the Minister for Education Donogh O'Malley announced the provision of free post-primary schooling. Free school transport was intended to facilitate attendance, which rose from 148,000 in 1967 to 185,000 in 1968–9. In October 1970, the government announced the creation of community schools. Building on the earlier comprehensive school structure, these would provide for adult education and be centres of learning for local communities.

The *Investment in Education Report* had revealed systemic omissions and, despite significant developments in the 1970s (such as the new primary curriculum (1971); establishment of management boards in primary schools (1975); and increased levels of participation at both levels) by the early 1980s, access to a post-primary education, in particular, remained limited. Radical measures remained absent. Early school leaving had not been seriously challenged; the legitimacy of the predominantly academic Leaving Certificate programme was popularly accepted; and access for children with learning difficulties was not part of educational discourse.

Developments in Education Policy and Practice: 1984–95

Gemma Hussey became Minister for Education in 1982 and set out to tackle a number of the issues that still existed. Conscious of the need for economic reform, changes in employment expectations and a wider dialogue concerning schooling, the Fine Gael government launched its *Programme for Action* in 1984. The programme emphasised the notion of access for all, insisting upon 'equal opportunities for educational advancement', and suggested that 'provision … discriminate positively in favour of the educationally disadvantaged'. For the first time, the place of women in educational management, the availability of subjects to girls and gender stereotyping in textbooks were addressed. Significantly, the document emphasised the relationship between the economy and schooling, stressing the need for the education system to 'respond to … increased mobility in the labour force'. *Programme for Action* established the tone of educational discourse for the next decade, as the issue of education for all became a constant in discussions about provision.

In 1990, the Fianna Fáil Minister for Education Mary O'Rourke initiated a consultation process on whether or not an Education Act was desirable, pointing to the 'disadvantaged' women and parents who were excluded from provision at ground, managerial and consultative levels. The government's draft Green Paper (1991) suggested linking school funding with admissions policy and suggested that it might 'explore' the funding of private schools. When the paper was published by O'Rourke's successor Séamus Brennan, it retained its emphasis upon disadvantage but also stressed the need to generate an 'enterprise' culture, prepare teachers for a more fluid social and economic environment, and seek means of ensuring standards and transparency.

When the Green Paper *Education for a Changing World* was published under Minister Niamh Bhreathnach in 1992, it emphasised the changing nature of global society and the need for schools to respond. The first of 'six key aims', however, was to 'establish greater equity in education … for those who are disadvantaged socially, economically, physically or mentally'. The paper pointed to the complexity of achieving greater equity and access, and stressed the need to create a 'home/school/community links project' combined with additional budgets for schools 'serving disadvantaged areas'.

The following year (1993), the Green Paper formed the basis of discussion for the National Education Convention, comprising over forty interested parties. The Background Paper to the Convention stressed that any inequality in terms of participation was unacceptable and commented that, in the 'interests of social justice', inequality needed to be addressed both within its 'wider social context and within the schools'. The paper also stressed the needs of children of the Travelling community and those with disabilities or special needs.

The discussion that had been taking place since the early 1990s culminated in 1995 with the publication of the White Paper *Charting our Education Future*. The paper submitted five pillars upon which policy should be developed:

- quality
- equality
- pluralism
- partnership
- accountability.

The state was obliged to 'seek to eliminate or compensate for … sources and consequences of educational disadvantage'. The document committed the government to 'allocating resources to those in greatest need' and to 'changing the system itself to cater for the diverse educational needs … of the population'.

The paper was timely given that, despite the vibrancy of Ireland's economy in the mid-1990s, over 2,000 children left post-primary school with no qualification and almost 8,000 left with Junior Certificate only. The right of children with special educational needs to access and participate at all levels was highlighted and schools were required to design strategies for the identification and assessment of – and to make plans for assistance of – such pupils. In particular, the paper emphasised the imperative of children attending mainstream schooling whenever possible. From the point of view of those teaching in traditional post-primary settings at the time, one of the paper's most striking assertions was that the 'traditional LC does not cater adequately for … needs and abilities of students …' and that there was an evident need to make the Leaving Certificate course provide for the 'holistic development of all students', thus empowering them to 'actively shape the social and economic future of society.'

Two direct consequences of this were the development of the Leaving Certificate Applied (LCA) and the Leaving Certificate Vocational Programme (LCVP). The former was designed to 'prepare students for the transition from school to adult and working life, including further education' and was to be introduced on a phased basis from September 1995. The LCVP programme would seek to 'foster skills … which assist young people to be successful as employees' and 'become entrepreneurs and employers'.

Regarding the teaching profession, the White Paper outlined the government's understanding of future needs. It promised induction for all teachers, but at the time of writing this has yet to come about. Those choosing to enter teaching should know that Ireland is almost alone within the European Community in failing to provide this service at a systematic level. Induction of new and beginning teachers is, therefore, left to the goodwill of individual schools; a situation the teaching profession must hope will be rectified sooner rather than later.

Much of the rhetoric of this period related to the need for teachers to adapt to the climate of 'accelerating change'. Central to the economic upturn of the mid-1990s was a series of social partnership agreements that impacted upon government expectations of the teaching profession in terms of the need for greater accountability and so-called quality assurance. The latter would lead directly to the present system of Whole School Evaluation. One of the strategies for facilitating greater transparency, accountability and effectiveness was the School Plan. Formal planning was already a well-established practice at primary level but uncommon in the post-primary community. The White Paper indicated that these schools would be obliged to develop a comprehensive plan and an annual report of the school's 'activities'. This plan was to become a key component in the process of

Whole School Evaluation and those entering the teaching profession would play a full part in the process.

THE EDUCATION ACT 1998

The 1992 Green and 1995 White papers resulted in the 1998 Education Act; the legislation under which schools and teachers operate. Those considering entering the teaching profession should familiarise themselves with its content.

In relation to the operation of schools, the act lays down directives in a number of areas. Recognised schools must provide education which is 'appropriate' to the 'ability and needs' of its pupils (para. 9: p. 13). Pupils must have access to guidance regarding career choices. Schools are bound to promote the moral, spiritual, social and personal development of pupils, and ensure equality of opportunity for both genders (pupils and staff). Schools should endeavour to promote the development of the Irish language. Parents should be granted access to all records pertaining to their child held by the school. Boards of Management and school principals are bound to ensure that staff development and the needs of management are provided for and to establish appropriate means of assessing the effectiveness of teaching and attainment. Importantly, schools should establish an admissions policy that provides for maximum accessibility.

SCHOOLS: MANAGEMENT AND OPERATION

Once employed, teachers operate under the auspices of the school's Board of Management and within the professional guidelines set down by the Teaching Council. If a teacher has obtained a permanent post, his/her salary is paid directly by the Department of Education and Science (DES). It is important that prospective teachers understand the role of the Board of Management. For many beginning teachers, the function of the board is somewhat mysterious and unless nominated as a staff representative, they have few dealings with it. However, the board is entrusted with significant responsibilities, including the hiring of new staff.

Principally, the duty of the board is to:

- manage the school on behalf of the patron
- be accountable for upholding the school ethos
- consult with and inform the school patron regarding decisions and proposals
- publish an admissions policy (including information pertaining to

expulsion, suspension, participation vis à vis disability and educational needs)

- have regard to the efficient use of resources in the operation of the school
- ensure that 'reasonable provision' is made for pupils with special needs.

It is the board's responsibility to establish procedures for informing parents about the operation and performance of the school as outlined in the School Plan and to ensure that the plan is prepared and circulated to the school patron, parents, teachers and staff. It is likely that, when an applicant is interviewed for a teaching post, the panel will include at least one member of the school Board of Management.

TYPES OF SCHOOL

There are three categories of post-primary school in Ireland:

1. Voluntary secondary schools.
2. Community and comprehensive schools.
3. Vocational schools.

Historically, culturally and in terms of provision and enrolment, these are often quite different institutions, reflecting a specific ethos and varying in operation, fees structure, management practices and subjects offered. As outlined above, the three types of institution have different historical antecedents and varying emphasis regarding vocational and traditional liberal education.

Voluntary Secondary Schools

The majority of schools in Ireland fall within this category. These schools have usually developed from religious and/or private institutions and remain privately owned and managed. They are state funded and usually do not charge fees. They are operated and managed by boards of governors, representatives of the relevant religious body or by individuals. The Joint Managerial Body for Secondary Schools, Ireland (JMB) represents voluntary secondary schools (www.jmb.ie).

Community and Comprehensive Schools

The founding principle of these schools is the provision of a comprehensive curriculum, combining traditional academic and technical/vocational education. They also provide adult education. They are publicly owned, are operated by boards of management and are wholly state funded. The Association of Community and Comprehensive Schools (ACCS) is the representative body for this sector (www.accs.ie).

Vocational Schools

As outlined above, vocational schools date from the 1930s, when a need was identified for the provision of a more technical and work-orientated curriculum. Vocational schools are publicly owned and funded and administered by local Vocational Education Committees (VECs). Despite the rationale on which these schools were originally founded, they have gradually widened provision to include both vocational education and the traditional academic curriculum. They have also developed a range of post-Leaving Certificate courses. They are represented by the Irish Vocational Education Association (IVEA) (www.ivea.ie).

Where to Work? Choosing a School

Often the nature of an undergraduate degree and initial teacher education qualification will influence the type of school in which a newly qualified teacher will seek work. However, graduates seeking teaching posts should consider the type of culture in which they would most like to work. Some may find the mixture offered by comprehensive or vocational schools more attractive than traditional voluntary schools, which they may perceive as narrow or limited in subject range. Others might be drawn to the tradition of learning and teaching offered by the voluntary sector or parts of it, such as the Jesuit, Holy Ghost or Dominican traditions.

It is important that aspiring teachers take cognisance of the differences between types of school and undertake some research into the type of institution in which they think they would be most comfortable. Schools are not the same. Apart from everyday challenges to do with classroom management, examinations, preparation and so on, schools develop individual cultures, usually, if not always, based upon their ethos and mission.

Those seeking work in a specific school should become familiar with its origin, ethos, management organisation and general pupil profile. They should seek to understand the context in which the school was founded and what it seeks to achieve. While the need to simply secure a post may be pressing, it is important, nonetheless, to understand the differences between types of school, which, after all, provide a tangible lesson in the development and evolution of schooling in Ireland.

THE TEACHING COUNCIL: QUALIFICATIONS AND REGISTRATION AS A POST-PRIMARY TEACHER

The most important recent development in relation to the operation, registration, practice and means of qualification for teachers is the establishment of the Teaching Council of Ireland. The council is a professional organisation principally made up of the teaching body and it aims to oversee the development of the profession. The Teaching Council operates under the Teaching Council Act 2001 and has far-ranging powers. A qualified teacher (the council stipulates the conditions for this) must register with the council in order to teach in Ireland. Student-teachers, or newly qualified teachers, should consult the Teaching Council of Ireland website for a comprehensive overview of its aims, objectives, authority and procedures (www.teachingcouncil.ie).

The purpose of the Teaching Council is to:

- regulate the profession
- identify and promote professional conduct
- establish and promote the maintenance and improvement of standards of programmes and courses for initial teacher education, and to review and accredit such programmes
- promote teaching as a profession
- publish and review codes of conduct/standards of, so-called, competence
- establish a register of teachers and procedures regarding the induction of new teachers
- inquire into and impose sanctions regarding fitness to teach.

The council comprises thirty-seven members: twenty-two nominated by teachers (primary and post-primary); two by initial teacher education institutions; four by school management organisations; two by national associations of parents; and five by the minister.

QUALIFICATION REQUIREMENTS FOR POST-PRIMARY TEACHERS

In order to practise as a post-primary teacher in Ireland, it is necessary to have completed a recognised primary degree and initial teacher education qualification (e.g. Postgraduate Diploma in Education). A recognised degree (or equivalent) is a degree awarded by a state-recognised university or third-level institution that allows the holder to teach one or more subjects from the post-primary curriculum to Leaving Certificate Higher Level.

While most undergraduate degrees are of three years' duration, there are a small number of three- and four-year initial teacher education undergraduate degrees that are discipline specific. These are offered at various universities and colleges in Ireland and cater, for example, for those wishing to teach Physical Education, Science, Art or Home Economics. A list of approved recognised subjects for post-primary teaching is available on the website of the Teaching Council of Ireland (www.teachingcouncil.ie/registration_information).

A recognised initial teacher education qualification may only be awarded from a State-recognised university or similar institution; it must prepare candidates to teach the post-primary age spectrum (twelve–eighteen); and be of at least one year's duration.

Uncertainty Regarding your Qualification

Occasionally, a candidate wishing to register as a post-primary teacher in Ireland discovers that his/her qualification is not recognised by the Teaching Council. It is important, before embarking on the application process, that candidates check the list of recognised qualifications. These are available on the Teaching Council of Ireland website (www.teachingcouncil.ie/registration_information). Candidates should note that the council will undertake individual assessment of qualifications if requested and the procedure for this is outlined on their website.

APPOINTMENTS TO TEACHING POSTS

Post-primary and VEC schools are allocated a quota of teaching posts in line with teacher–pupil ratios. Recent graduates should be aware that it is unusual to secure a publicly funded, permanent post upon qualification. Very often, graduates will obtain 'hours' on a privately paid basis before eventually securing a permanent post. The contractual obligations in such instances are those that relate to all legal contracts concerning employment, but it should be noted that such a contract is between the individual and the school; the Department of Education and Science is not party to the contract. Teachers should be aware of their statutory rights and obligations regarding pension contributions, holiday pay, sick leave and so on, when entering such a contract.

Publicly funded teaching posts are advertised in the public press and it is important that newly qualified teachers keep a close eye on these notices, particularly during the early summer months. The selection of a candidate for a post, regardless of its nature (permanent whole-time, temporary whole-time or part-time), is the responsibility of the individual school. Regardless of which sector of the education system a candidate wishes to work in (VEC, voluntary secondary, etc.), all prospective teachers must fulfil the registration conditions as outlined by the Teaching Council of Ireland in relation to:

- A recognised degree.
- A recognised initial teacher-education qualification.
- Having undertaken the required number of school-based teaching practice hours (100 hours).

Teacher Remuneration

Teachers are paid on the basis of a common incremental salary. There are also a number of allowances, including those related to degrees and initial teacher-education diplomas/degrees. Salary scales change over time and the DES provides an up-to-date summary on its website (www.education.ie).

Specialist Teaching Posts

Those seeking to secure a specialist teaching post must hold the required qualifications for registration as a post-primary teacher coupled with a recognised qualification in the specialist area. The Teaching Council sets out three such areas:

- Learning support teacher.
- Special educational needs teacher.
- Guidance counsellor.

Courses Pertaining to Learning Support Teachers

The following institutions offer postgraduate qualifications in the area of Learning Support that are recognised by the Department of Education and Science.

- Church of Ireland College of Education, Dublin – Diploma in Learning Support.
- Department of Education, NUI Cork – Higher Diploma in Learning Support.
- Department of Education, NUI Galway – Higher Diploma in Learning Support.
- Mary Immaculate College, Limerick – Graduate Diploma in Learning Support.

Courses Pertaining to Special Needs Teaching
- Church of Ireland of Education, Dublin – Diploma in Special Education Needs.
- Mary Immaculate College, Limerick – Postgraduate/Master's in Special Educational Needs.
- NUI, Dublin – Higher Diploma in Remedial and Special Education.
- St Angela's College, Sligo – Higher Diploma in Special Education Needs.

The following institutions offer postgraduate qualifications in the area of Special Education Needs that are recognised by the Department of Education and Science.

- NUI, Dublin – Higher Diploma in Remedial and Special Education.
- St Angela's College, Sligo – Higher Diploma in Special Education Needs.
- Church of Ireland College of Education, Dublin – Diploma in Special Education Needs.
- Mary Immaculate College, Limerick – Graduate Diploma in Special Education Needs.
- St Patrick's College, Dublin – Diploma in Education (Special/Inclusive Education) (online course).

Courses Pertaining to Guidance Counselling
The following institutions offer postgraduate qualifications in the area of Guidance Counselling that are recognised by the Department of Education and Science.

- Dublin City University – Graduate Diploma/MSc in Guidance and Counselling.
- NUI, Cork – Higher Diploma in Guidance and Counselling.
- NUI, Maynooth – Higher Diploma in Guidance and Counselling.
- University of Dublin – Master's Degree in Education (Guidance and Counselling)/MSc Degree in Educational Guidance and Counselling.
- University of Limerick – Postgraduate Diploma in Guidance Counselling.
- Marino Institute of Education, Dublin – Master's Degree in Family Counselling.

Applying for the Postgraduate Diploma in Education
The Postgraduate Diploma in Education is offered by the following third-level institutions.

- Dublin City University (a part-time, two-year course).

- National University of Ireland, Galway.
- National University of Ireland, Maynooth.
- National University of Ireland, Cork.
- National University of Ireland, Dublin.
- National University of Ireland, Limerick.
- University of Dublin (Trinity College).

Applicants wishing to apply for the Postgraduate Diploma in Education should apply to:

> The Postgraduate Applications Centre
> First Floor
> Tower House
> Eglinton Street
> Galway
> Republic of Ireland
> Telephone:(+353/0) 91 509817
> Website: www.pac.ie

Applicants wishing to undertake the diploma at the National University of Ireland, Limerick, or the University of Dublin (Trinity College) should apply directly to those colleges.

2

Beginning Well: Initial Considerations for ITE

Brendan Walsh

THE THEORY AND PRACTICE OF TEACHING

Regardless of the type of teacher education degree or diploma for which you are studying, there are a number of common features and requirements that you need to bear in mind. All such programmes are very demanding and, in Ireland, they can vary in duration from one to four years (see Chapter 1). While primary schoolteachers have traditionally undergone a four-year preparatory degree, there are now, in Ireland, a number of four-year degree programmes for post-primary teachers, for example, in Science and Physical Education.

From the outset, the student-teacher should understand the nature of these programmes and be quite clear that total engagement with their content is essential in order to begin to master the craft of teaching. Traditionally, student-teachers have been eager to acquire a set of 'skills' that will enable them to function in a classroom setting. They are anxious about discipline, content and being 'effective'. Only slowly do they begin to realise that they are becoming educators rather than teachers and that this is a complex and multifaceted task.

The authors of this book have found that student-teachers without experience of teaching are anxious to learn about classroom management (discipline) and evaluation (testing), while those with two or more years of experience want to learn more about these areas but are eager to acquire a wider and deeper knowledge of education as a professional engagement. Disciplines such as Psychology, Curriculum Studies, History, Sociology and Methodology support and inform practice, helping to foster a broader appreciation. While they may not seem immediately relevant, they form the essential pillars upon which all student-teachers must build their professional practice. They help to induct the teacher into the community of education specialists and enable them to understand the wider implications and complexities of teaching.

Student-teachers sometimes report that their more experienced colleagues in school can be less than convinced about the relationship between the theory of teaching and its practice. This undermines teaching because it implies that it is a professional practice without theoretical foundations, making it a task that can be engaged in so long as a person has acquired a set of 'skills' or competencies. Student-teachers should clearly understand the integral relationship between educational theory and practice. The theoretical enriches our understanding of the practical and ultimately enhances teaching and, therefore, pupil learning. It is essential that student teachers successfully combine the demands of teaching practice with the rigour of academic work; that they engage wholeheartedly and meaningfully with course work, practicals and workshops. A person cannot learn to teach simply by trial and error in a classroom. The implications of such an attitude towards the learner are obvious.

COLLEGE: PREPARATION AND ENGAGEMENT

When you have begun your course, it is important that you familiarise yourself with your college and department. The administrator or tutor will help you with this. You should locate the relevant sections in the library early in the academic year and begin following up recommended reading as soon as possible. The demands of teaching placement mean that you will not have much spare time on your hands and you need to organise your time to allow for lectures, course work and tutorials. This is a very obvious difference between the postgraduate diploma and undergraduate degree courses and student-teachers should realise from the outset that, as a rule, the pace and intensity of the diploma limits opportunities for study and reading. Consequently, it is important to discover what is needed and where to locate it as early in the course as possible.

THE SCHOOL VISIT

Either before or upon beginning your course, you may be asked to make a preliminary visit to the school where you will undertake your teaching placement. This visit is important and you should ensure that you have all the information required to make the most of it.

Some student-teachers may be asked to undergo an observation week before beginning. Usually, this involves sitting in on lessons and observing experienced teachers. If you are required to undertake an observation week, you should ensure that it is an opportunity for learning and meaningful observation. If it is in the same school that is hosting your teaching placement, you should also familiarise yourself with how the school operates. For example, you might request a copy of the school rules and regulations, find out about its history, the subjects it offers, its ethos and so on.

The Initial School Visit: Factors to Consider

If you are only required to pay a once-off initial visit to your host school, you should be consider the following. Regardless of whether or not your department has arranged this visit, you should, as a matter of courtesy, phone in good time ahead of your visit to remind the school administrator of the appointment and arrange a set time to arrive. Do not be late and if you should be held up, contact the school as soon as possible. Upon arrival, call at the school's reception desk, introduce yourself and explain that you are expected.

It is important that you dress correctly for this visit. Generally, be conservative in your attire at this stage, regardless of the culture of the school. As you will probably be meeting the principal, it is important that you make a good first impression. It is helpful if you have done some research about the school before your visit, are familiar with its ethos, size, interests (sport, drama, debating, etc.) and the subjects it offers. You may have acquired the school prospectus, which will provide you not only with general information but also enable you to pinpoint areas about which you wish to make enquires. Bringing this with you will demonstrate your interest and professionalism.

The principal, vice-principal and subject/co-operating teacher will have expectations about what they want you to do, but this should not prevent you from asking questions. In particular, you should be clear about what you will be expected to teach and to whom. You should also seek information on school policy regarding discipline, roll call, the use of resources, allocation of classrooms, access to equipment, record keeping, homework allocation and evaluation.

Be prepared, if your timetable permits, to volunteer for extracurricular activities. Schools are always interested in what student-teachers can contribute and you should be willing to become involved. If you have a background in football, drama, debating, etc., you should inform the school and be prepared to help out in school activities. However, a word of warning – student-teachers have many demands on their time and if you are asked to commit to extracurricular activities, you need to ensure that it is not unreasonable. The school should understand that you have many commitments and you may need to outline them, gently, if you are faced with too many requests.

During your visit to the school ask to see the room in which you will be teaching: this will give you a mental picture of the space available to you when you are planning. You can also identify any possible difficulties you may encounter because of a lack of space, poor lighting, background noise or crowding. Try to get a sense of the building, where the administration office, photocopying room, staff room and bathrooms are, and, if possible, take a walk around the building. It is not uncommon for pupils to be less than truthful with new teachers about how long it took them to walk to class or what room they are coming from; a good sense of the school building will help you spot any inconsistencies.

Do not be afraid to ask questions. The principal, or co-operating teacher, will be reassured by your engagement and willingness to gather the information necessary to make a good beginning. If you are teaching subjects that require apparatus, such as Geography, Science, Technical Drawing, Woodwork or Metalwork, make sure you know where the apparatus is kept and what regulations govern its distribution and use. If you have not bought a *Teacher Journal*, do so, and, if available, ask for the relevant class lists and timetable. The journal is designed around the teaching year and is an invaluable aid.

When you are happy that you have gathered all the required information, check that you know what date and time you are required to be at school to begin teaching.

Observing Experienced Teachers Teaching

Some teacher education degrees/diplomas require student teachers to observe experienced teachers before beginning teaching practice. This is a very useful exercise, although when undertaken within the first week or two of the student-teachers' academic year, they may be unsure to what to look for and there are good reasons for encouraging them to observe later in the year, when their understanding of the challenges and possibilities of teaching have become more sophisticated.

Student-teachers are, initially, faced with a number of common challenges, in particular:

- classroom management
- appropriate pitching of content

- lesson pacing and maintaining pupil interest.

These are dealt with elsewhere in this book but, during observation, you should seek to identify the specific ways in which experienced teachers deal with the complexities of lesson presentation and pupil learning.

Do not be surprised to find significant differences in how teachers approach these matters. Teaching is a highly individual and complex activity. A multitude of factors influence each lesson, including:

- time of day
- personality
- subject matter
- presentation
- methodology
- teacher and pupil disposition
- location
- classroom environment
- group dynamic.

Each teacher develops his/her own distinctive 'style'. Often, student-teachers model their teaching on teachers they admired while they were in school. This is usual, but you should be reassured that you will develop your own approaches and dispositions and that you will become the teacher you were meant to be, bringing your own talents, expertise, disposition and sympathy to the task.

When observing experienced teachers, it is important that you remain aware of how pupils respond and behave. If they are actively engaged, you should ask yourself what the teacher is doing that is prompting this response. Pay attention to seemingly mundane activities, such as how the experienced teacher moves about the room, makes eye contact with pupils, employs the blackboard or a resource, makes changes in his/her tone of voice and gesture, uses anecdote and humour, and reacts to pupil misbehaviour. Also observe how the pace of the lesson varies according to pupil comprehension and content.

Many aspects of good teaching, of creating a work-orientated co-operative atmosphere, are 'hidden'. Inflexions of voice, subtle gestures, movement, gentle refocusing of pupil attention and casual humour all work to create occasions for learning. You should, therefore, be sensitive to the seemingly ordinary actions of the experienced teacher; it is these fluid, almost imperceptible ways of operating that hold the lesson together, giving it rhythm and direction.

If you have an opportunity to speak with the teacher after an observed lesson make sure you have specific questions, but do not be disappointed if s/he has difficulty explaining exactly why or how elements of the lesson worked so well. Experienced teachers develop an array of dispositions and approaches, many of which are intuitive and have evolved through experiment and practice. This craft knowledge is invaluable to student-teachers and you should analyse their teaching carefully and try to identify what worked and why. If possible, you should observe different teachers at work and in subjects other than your own. Different disciplines demand varying approaches and exposure to them will help you understand just how wide this body of expertise can be.

Observation, then, should be reflective and active. Do not expect to somehow assemble a set of 'skills' that will prepare you for teaching. The complexity of the engagement means that you need to reflect on its variables, and attempt to distinguish between what would and would not be appropriate for you and your pupils. Ultimately, there is no prescriptive set of rules or 'skills' that can be applied to all teachers. Situations vary so widely that this is not possible. Certain common characteristics enable us to formulate general principles of practice, but, finally, each teacher develops the approaches that work best for him/her and his/her pupils. This can be disconcerting for student-teachers seeking a 'skills pack' that will enable them to become 'effective'. But, upon reflection, it is liberating. Each of us, in our own school, with our own dispositions and our own pupils, develops a manner and approach that works, and that is all that matters.

PLANNING FOR TEACHING

When you have completed your initial school visit and, hopefully, have had an opportunity to observe, you will need to start planning your scheme of work and lessons. We will return to these in greater detail later (see Chapter 3).

When beginning teaching practice, student-teachers sometimes face two specific challenges.

First, they find that they are not suitably familiar with course content. This may be because they have not encountered it at degree level – after all, these courses are obviously not tailored to meet the requirement of the post-primary school curriculum, nor should they be! It is important, therefore, that students ensure that they have mastered content before they begin teaching. There is no room for partial understandings: pupils have a right to expect that you are prepared, and inexplicable gaps in your knowledge will lead them to feel frustrated and suspicious.

Second, student-teachers can experience difficulties in pitching content at an appropriate level for their pupils. While making sure to ascertain previous pupil learning, it is important to remember that, usually, your pupils are aged between thirteen and seventeen. They are young and you should be slow to take their knowledge for granted. Try to imagine your own grasp of the subject at that age. They are still being exposed to a world of new ideas, vocabulary and possibilities, so you should not be surprised to find that they know little about the things you take for granted. You are there to induct them, to introduce and facilitate, not to simply 'pour' your knowledge into their heads! Of course, it is wise to talk to your pupils about prior knowledge of the subject, but, when planning, remember that they are being exposed to the complexities of your discipline, or aspects of it, for the first time.

When you have ascertained what you will be teaching, and have mastered its content, you will need to plan for the year. This is dealt with in Chapter 3 (page 29) and is an essential step in ensuring that you 'cover' the course. You should give some thought to evaluating learning, consider which parts of the course will be tested and how. You should also familiarise yourself with relevant workbooks and resources to be employed – it is advisable that you complete workbook exercises first to ensure that you understand the challenges that pupils will face.

Classroom Management: Initial Considerations

You should also, at this planning stage, give some thought to classroom management, an aspect of teaching that most student teachers find very challenging. You should be reassured that almost all student-teachers find pupil discipline difficult. Think for a moment of your time in school and the prospect of having a 'trainee' teacher as a substitute – surely visions of shoaling piranha come to mind!

First Thoughts on Classroom Management

Classroom management is a complex issue and student-teachers should accept, from the outset, that there are no simple solutions to indiscipline. It is a matter of trying and trying again; of effort, confidence building, firmness, fairness and goodwill.

In the beginning, however, you should decide on three or four simple, basic rules upon which you will insist. These will vary between teachers and will often be dictated by the type of school in which they are undertaking their practice. For example, rules around a student raising his/her hand before asking a question, not speaking out of turn, entering and exiting the classroom or having homework completed may be essential for one teacher. However, in a school where these principles are accepted, a teacher may design rules around treatment of equipment, inter-personal relationships and issues of respect and punctuality.

While teachers have different emphases, it is important that their regulations do not contradict wider school policy and, as always, are designed to enhance learning. This point is crucial. Regulations should not be arbitrary. Pupils should see that they exist to protect their freedom to learn and are, therefore, established upon respect for them and their aspirations.

It is important at the outset to understand that good working relationships with pupils are earned and should be founded on fairness, reasonableness and the need to create an environment in which all are free to learn and progress. The student-teacher should expect challenges in this area but remember that you should not expect adult behaviour from children, or even adolescents. Often, it is the daily and seemingly trivial forms of poor behaviour that are most wearing for teachers and it is essential that you develop a sense of perspective and humour in dealing with them.

When beginning, student-teachers are usually anxious to appear approachable and friendly. An old adage warns not to smile 'till Easter'! This is, perhaps, overstating the need to be stern, but there is a grain of truth in the caution. Good working relationships are built on pupils' understanding the nature of what it is you are there to actually do – to help them learn. They expect you to create an environment in which this is not only possible, but forms the very heart of your approach. Hence, they expect you to deal, firmly and fairly, with obstructions. Pupils do not expect to 'get away' with poor behaviour, they expect you, the adult, to intervene, assist and redirect them, and, if necessary, to take whatever action is needed to help them refocus on the work in hand.

Therefore, from the outset you must, in a clear, calm and reasonable manner, explain to pupils what you expect from them and the consequences of their failing to co-operate. In this way, there is complete clarity around how you operate and how lessons are to proceed.

You must, at the first instance of misbehaviour, remind pupils of what you expect and calmly implement whatever action you deem appropriate. Remember, you have already explained the regulations to the pupils at the beginning of the year, so, in effect, by misbehaving, a pupil is inviting the reprimand/action upon him/herself. We will return to this topic later (see Chapter 6), but, for now, it is important that your expectations are reasonable and clear and that you understand that pupils are not automata, that there will be challenges and that you must be prepared to deal with them with firmness but also a sense of perspective. After all, misbehaviour is seldom meant in a personal way, it is you as 'teacher', rather than you as 'person', at whom the poor behaviour is directed.

Striking the Right Balance: Managing your Time

We mentioned earlier that student-teachers have many demands upon their time and they should be careful not to accept duties and work that add significantly to their load. It is important to realise at the outset that, regardless of the length of the teaching practice placement or initial teacher educating degree/diploma, the process is arduous and tiring.

For many, teaching placement is the first experience of the professional workplace and the responsibility of teaching for the first time is daunting. Teaching is a rather lonely occupation. Teachers spend the majority of their day separated from their colleagues, in closed rooms, dealing with large numbers of pupils of various ages and dispositions.

When we begin teaching, the demands of the classroom are seemingly all-encompassing and it is common for student-teachers to complain of extreme tiredness. This is due to a number of factors. In the first instance, there is a certain nervousness that is in itself quite wearing. Then there are demands around getting 'up to speed' with content knowledge, textbooks, setting tests, and correcting assignments and homework. Indiscipline, especially if it is of a very challenging nature, can add significantly to the burden. Involvement in an array of extracurricular activities can also place demands on time, although these can be a good way of dealing with stress while also getting to know pupils in a different working context.

These demands must be balanced with those of college/university – the need to complete assignments, attend lectures and tutorials and find time for study. Also there may be personal, family or work demands that require attention. It is important, therefore, that you find an acceptable balance.

Your teaching placement is the key element of the degree/diploma and it is imperative that you are fully committed to it. However, it is also vital that you find time and space for leisure and relaxation. All too often, student-teachers fall into the trap of preparing schoolwork late into the evening and at weekends. While this may, occasionally, be necessary, it should not become the norm. You have a duty to yourself and those who care for you to avoid becoming wholly engrossed and while your family and friends will be willing to share the burden, it is important that you make time for them, and for you, to relax.

Pacing

The teaching day, indeed the teaching life, eventually takes on a certain rhythm. This is most evident in the way teachers approach certain parts of the curriculum and tasks at certain times of the year. Teachers intuitively develop a finely honed sense of pacing, in relation not just to the school year, but also to the teaching day.

As with any onerous task, it is difficult to maintain the same energy towards the end of the teaching day that was there at the beginning. This does not mean that those pupils we teach in late afternoon are somehow at a disadvantage. Rather, teaching demands the development of an overview of the day and an appropriate sense of pace. Regardless of the demands of the morning, we deliver our lessons at an even pace, aware that we need to give as generously at the end of the day as at the beginning.

Some groups will be more demanding and this enables us to vary our pace as others are simply less demanding, more co-operative and more engaged. This does not mean we do not fully commit to the lesson; rather, we deliver it in a manner that is appropriate to the group. Hence, a very motivated group will often be more enjoyable and less demanding; in a sense we can relax in this environment, knowing we will not have to expend energy on behaviour or learning issues. In this way, we learn that we do not need to go 'full tilt' with every group in the same way. Our teaching of a highly motivated group will be just as effective; it simply demands a different level of energy. It is important that student teachers try to develop this sense of pacing – otherwise they find that, by the afternoon, they are tired, lessons suffer and discipline issues appear worse than they actually are.

SECTION TWO
– THE CLASSROOM

3

Preparation and Planning

Brendan Walsh

THE YEARLY SCHEME OF WORK

The purpose of the Yearly Scheme is to enable student-teachers to plan the long-term teaching and learning requirements for their classes. Its aim is to ensure that they teach the full range of content and learn to arrange their teaching load to allow for holidays, examinations and revision time.

It is vital that, at the earliest possible stage, you ascertain which topics you will be teaching and plan for the coming year. You may break this into units according to months or themes but the end result should be that you have thought out your teaching for the year and know what you will be teaching to whom and when. In effect, the scheme should span the period between the beginning and the end of teaching practice. In reality, this may prove difficult. For example, you may not have been told what to teach after Christmas or Easter, but, in September, you should be able to plan for the first term at least. It is crucial that you are able to visualise and plan a coherent sequence of lessons that belong within a structured whole.

The scheme does not have to contain details of methodology, aims or objectives. It should simply represent what will be taught and when, although it is very useful to give some thought at this stage to the different demands the various topics will pose. It is essential that you ascertain what your pupils have already learned and arrange to discuss this with the class teacher as soon as possible. S/he will tell you what needs to be taught and will provide you with information about the groups and their learning to date. It is important that you allow yourself to be directed by the class teacher. However, this should not prevent you from bringing ideas to him/her concerning methodology, presentation and resources. The scheme may, for good reason, have to be altered in the course of the year and you should be flexible when requested or when the classroom dynamic demands it. This may occur, for example, where you have erroneously taken pupils' previous knowledge for granted and have had to reshuffle your scheme in order to allow for re-teaching or revision.

Increasingly, school departments design yearly schemes on a collaborative basis and teachers elect to teach particular units, themes or content. If this is so, you should ensure that you are included in this discussion and make it known if you are uncertain about the content allocated to you. This is important as pupils, parents or colleagues will not thank you if you elect to teach a course in which you are less than competent.

The scheme, then, is an essential organisational tool. It enables you to plan for the year or term in a sequential manner, ensuring that the entire course is taught and evaluated. It should reflect a coherent whole. The teaching year, in effect, is divided by the content you must teach and each part is allocated its specific time. This way, you can ensure that there is no cramming, no oversights and no time-wasting.

THE CO-OPERATING TEACHER: WORKING IN PARTNERSHIP

The responsibility of the co-operating teacher is to act as a guide and support to you during your teaching practice year. Schools differ in the emphasis they place on this role and the nominated teacher may not always be available to assist you. Schools are busy places and your co-operating teacher may have to deal with any number of important tasks. It remains uncommon for the nominated teacher to observe, or 'sit in', on student-teacher lessons. This should not stop you from requesting that s/he do so occasionally. Again, the nominated teacher might sit in at different phases of the lesson. For example, if you are experiencing difficulties getting the class to settle at the beginning of the lesson, s/he might observe this phase. It is important, however, that the nominated teacher sits in on your lessons whenever possible and that you seek advice and guidance on your teaching and the pupils' learning.

Schools differ in approach, ethos and character and it is important that you discuss these with your co-operating teacher. You should also be sure to gain as much information as you can about the groups, individuals and lessons you will be teaching. You will need to know if your pupils pose any specific challenges, the extent of their previous learning and whether or not there are pupils with particular learning difficulties. It is important that you are furnished with a comprehensive picture of what you are facing.

Your co-operating teacher can also help you locate material and resource;

this is particularly important in subjects such as Art and Science where materials are often potentially hazardous and kept under lock and key. In schools where groups have a designated classroom, you should enquire about furniture arrangements. Often, items are arranged in a particular way for good reason and you should consult the co-operating teacher before making changes. If you do rearrange seating, be sure to return it to its original layout before leaving the room. Check before borrowing or using equipment and be careful not to disturb material, folders, books and so on that the co-operating teacher has filed away. As a general rule, while bearing the authority and responsibilities of a permanent member of staff, you must also remember that you are a guest in a host school and the usual professional courtesies apply.

The co-operating teacher's most important role, however, is that of mentor. S/he, by virtue of inviting you into his/her classroom and giving you the responsibility of teaching, has a responsibility to act as guide and support. This is not an evaluative role and student-teachers should be prepared, indeed anxious, to benefit from the co-operating teacher's knowledge, experience and insight. The enormous body of 'craft-knowledge' possessed by a collective staff is often under-utilised by student-teachers and you should be open to suggestions, advice and direction.

Traditionally, student-teachers are inclined to seek help when faced with challenges, particularly classroom management. However, you should seek to share ideas on methodology, resources and evaluation with your co-operating teacher. S/he will advise you on the merits, or otherwise, of what you are planning and will offer invaluable suggestions on modifications to suit particular groups. You should feel free to discuss your lesson plans, tests, homework allocation and correction with the co-operating teacher and be prepared to make modifications if necessary.

OBSERVING AND BEING OBSERVED: 'SITTING IN' ON LESSONS

If possible, you should observe your co-operating teacher teaching. This is an invaluable source of ideas and, when faced with challenges, a wonderful reassurance. Some student-teachers express concern about allowing a colleague 'sit in' as they feel this will undermine their authority with the group. Class groups generally know which members of staff are student-teachers and, usually, this is in no way counterproductive. Indeed, the appearance of a younger teacher can be a refreshing experience for them.

The importance of 'sitting in' lies in the experienced teacher being observed in an everyday environment. You can see how s/he deals with situations or elements you find challenging. In particular, you should be aware of his/her tone of voice, the pace of the lesson, physical movement in the room, the manner in which questions are asked and responded to, the routines and phases of the lesson, how information is elicited and prompts given. In short, you should observe, in a reflective manner, and attempt to discover what it is that makes the lesson flow in an even and learning-orientated way as, often, this is due to unremarkable, invisible and intuitive actions on the part of the experienced teacher.

Your observation should enable you make comparisons with your own practice and result in a shortlist of changes you might make, which should be simple and achievable. For example, you might decide that your lesson will not begin until there is silence, or that you will remember to check for homework not presented on the previous day. Resolutions such as 'I will have better classroom management' or 'I will ask better questions' are of little use as they are too general. You should decide on the type of questions you need to ask. For example, should there be a better combination of lower- and higher-order and of open and closed questions? Will you accept limited answers or probe for greater comprehension? If possible, the student-teacher should meet with the co-operating teacher after an observed lesson to discuss those aspects the former found most useful and to seek clarity on how the co-operating teacher managed the various challenges that arose.

You should remember, however, that teachers are faced with a wide range of demands. They often operate in immensely challenging environments that are difficult and tiring. At different stages, they are engaged in preparing pupils for state and school examinations. It is not unusual for teachers to revert to conservative, pragmatic teaching styles during these periods. Student-teachers should recognise that different styles may be required at different times to achieve different results, and see these as occasions for learning and developing as teachers. Again, they should be reassured that inventive, adventurous and unorthodox teaching and good examination results are not, by any means, mutually exclusive.

It is important that 'sitting in' continues throughout the student-teacher's placement as, often, student-teachers do not, initially, know what to look for and it is only as they progress and experience different challenges and groups that observation begins to be a genuinely helpful experience. In this way, the student-teacher begins to realise that teaching is a complicated endeavour. What works for one teacher may not work for another. It may also be reassuring to discover that experienced colleagues face similar challenges and that, sometimes, they too have to begin again and find new ways of approaching both subject and pupils.

If possible, the student-teacher should observe more than one teacher, as teaching styles can differ greatly but are nonetheless equally effective. This can be frustrating for the student-teacher looking for a set of methods or a particular way of doing things that simply *works*, but the realisation that there are as many styles as there are teachers should be liberating.

Ultimately, teaching is a deeply human endeavour and each teacher moulds the demands teaching brings according to his/her talents, disposition and character. Observation, then, should lead to reflection on how your teaching can improve, but central to this should be how your teaching will enhance pupil learning. Regardless of the multitude of resources employed, the range and type of questions or the complexity of the lesson plan, it is pupil learning, rather then teacher performance, that is at the heart of schooling.

LESSON PLANNING

Mixed Ability Groups

The term 'mixed ability' is contentious. Cohen and Manion (1983:89–90) note that 'it is quite impossible to discuss the topic ... without bearing in mind that the term has different meanings for different people'. Generally 'mixed ability' refers to pupil groupings comprising children with a range of abilities and aptitudes. Unless a group is rigidly 'streamed' or 'banded' according to an apparent common level, and even within this there will be significant variations, all groups will include a wide range of abilities.

However, many groups are taught as if no such variation exists and lessons are pitched to an imagined middle-ground. Such an approach is profoundly counterproductive, and its antecedents lie in the historic understanding of teaching as 'mug and jug' – the filling of empty heads. In this respect, schoolteachers have taught groups in much the same way for more than a century and many would argue – given pupil–teacher ratios, the demands of state examinations, school resourcing, the consensualist nature of the curriculum and the absence of continued professional development for teachers – that there is no practical alternative.

While it is important that student-teachers understand the limitations in which schooling operates, this should not prevent them from striving to engage with their pupils in inventive and individualistic ways. It is incumbent upon them to ascertain the various abilities of their pupils. A useful guide for this is to look at the pupils' scores in previous tests. This is not always reliable, as will be discussed below, but it can provide the new teacher with a rough guide. An unorthodox but useful approach can be to simply discuss subject matter with a group and ask them what they consider their level of comprehension to be. This can work very well with older groups and motivated pupils.

Usually, teachers prepare and present lessons in a teacher-centred manner; that is, they speak to an attentive and usually silent group. Interaction is limited and pupils are understood as passive and receptive. This is not unlike the lecture format where information is delivered and it is assumed the listeners are internalising it in a reflective manner.

While this format is the basis for much teaching, it is usual for teachers to prompt an exchange of views or seek information from the group. This may be aimed at ensuring comprehension, prompting pupils to articulate more complex understandings of material, or initiating a whole group discussion around an issue or topic. This approach may lend itself to pupils' interaction in the form of assistance, qualification of remarks, disagreements about topics, themes or opinions.

This type of interaction, when focused and guided, can become a wonderful occasion for learning. Indeed, it is very rewarding to oversee pupils exchange views that are embedded in a sound understating of the content being taught. It represents their taking ownership of the material and reflects their personal engagement with it. It is important, however, that such discussions remain grounded in the topic and that opinions can be supported using the material under discussion, be that a poem, experiment or historical event. The danger for the student-teacher is that pupils can introduce 'red herrings' and even try to prise inappropriate information from the teacher or other pupils. The key to success then, is to remain subject-focused and keep the discussion moving toward a predetermined outcome, while allowing for the occasional cul-de-sac, which can, if sensibly handled, become part of the learning process!

This co-operative forum works well with motivated pupils, but it should not be neglected when dealing with less enthusiastic groups. It may be the case that they have not previously been invited to engage in such a discussion. So long as it remains focused and directed towards predetermined learning, there is no reason not to employ this style. Giving pupils a sense of ownership over the material gives them greater confidence and often results in their becoming more engaged with the subject content.

Lesson Planning: Initial Considerations

Teachers employ some or all of the above methods in every lesson, usually beginning with lecture-style explanation, moving on to questioning, prompting a discussion and ending with a lecture-style summary. When planning lessons, you must consider the style or styles you wish to employ. At this stage, it is important to point out that you should not feel tied to any one style or plan. Beginning teaching is a balancing act between the safety of good lesson planning and preparation and the seemingly choppy but wonderful waters of full-blown teacher–pupil engagement. So, before discussing lesson planning, it is important to remember the following.

Models of planning vary considerably. As a rule, no model is better than another and student-teachers should be prepared to adopt the model that best suits them, their teaching style and the pupils they teach. Plans should not be understood as 'written in stone': what appears as a sensible way of approaching this or that topic may turn out to be misjudged. It is very common for student-teachers to report that the plan did not 'work' with this group or that topic. This may be because of any number of factors, but, ultimately, it is a great learning experience: the teacher, not the plan, teaches the lesson.

Teaching according to your plan means finding the correct balance between ensuring that your pupils actually engage with the material and that verifiable learning takes place (presuming that this is one of your objectives!) and being able to allow other, equally valid learning outcomes to occur. The plan should be understood as a foundation, a road map for your lesson, but it should never exclude the possibility of exploring other avenues of learning. Be prepared, therefore, to allow for occasions to develop that lead to intelligent engagement and, when the time is right, gently coach your pupils back to the requirements of your overall plan.

You should plan every lesson. In the same way that a pilot goes through a standard procedure before every flight, teachers must plan each lesson. With time, this becomes easier and can be done in a very short space of time.

The importance of planning, especially for the student-teacher, cannot be overemphasised. The old adage 'fail to plan, plan to fail' is true on a number of levels in teaching. In particular, poor planning can lead to disruption. Vague, meandering and uncertain teaching leads to disengagement and pupils will be tempted to fill gaps by other means. A well-paced, work-oriented, subject-focused plan will do much to ensure attention and engagement. But planning is not a management tool. Good planning is designed to enhance learning opportunities. Its fundamental aim and purpose is to help pupils learn; that is what they expect.

Good planning also enables the student teacher to be more confident about the lesson. S/he knows what has to be done, how it is to be done and what the end result should be. S/he has reviewed the content and is confident s/he understands it. Good planning enables the student teacher to have confident ownership of the material and this empowers him/her in the classroom. This confidence and mastery goes a long way, often without the student teacher realising it, to minimising disruption, fostering engagement and increasing interest in the subject matter.

Preparing a Lesson Plan

There are a number of elements common to all lesson planning. The following must be included in any plan.

Educational/Learning Objectives
1. The overall aim of the lesson.
2. The objectives of the lesson.
3. The content of the lesson.
4. The activities that will comprise the lesson.
5. The resources to be employed.
6. The evaluation of learning.
7. Critical reflection and resolutions.

The overall aim of the lesson

It is essential that the student teacher has a clear understanding of the purpose of the lesson. S/he must know precisely what it is s/he wants the pupils to do/learn. There must be no ambiguity about this. Vague aspirations such as 'the pupils will learn about how the presence of rivers impacts upon human settlement' are of little use. While the aims are later broken down into objectives, it is still important that you are very clear on the precise aim of a lesson. The above aim, for example, might be rendered as 'the pupils will learn how rivers impact upon human settlement under the following headings: historic settlement; trade and transport; human settlement; defence; industry; and urban growth'. This way, the teacher ensures that the essential elements are covered and pupils can see relationships between them.

The aim may be for a unit of lessons centred upon a wider theme or topic. For example, a series of lessons on the poetry of the First World War might have as its aim: 'An understanding of the forms, language and imagery of the war employed by war poets coupled with an appreciation of the themes of: innocence; futility; comradeship; heroism; and pacifism.' Aims must be designed with the demands of the syllabus and subject discipline, and the ability of the pupils, in mind. A course such as the above may be taught to two different groups and the level at which it is pitched may vary considerably.

When planning aims, the student-teacher should consider previous knowledge or learning. If it is an entirely new topic, s/he should include a generous introduction in order to contextualise the unit and outline its direction and his/her expectations. S/he must also consider how the learning will be evaluated and what methods and learning activities should be employed in teaching the unit or lesson. It is important at the outset that the student-teacher becomes accustomed to reflecting upon these areas. After a while, they will become an instinctive part of planning, but, in the early stages, the student-teacher should have a checklist to ensure these elements have been considered.

The objectives of the lesson

The objectives of a lesson are the learning outcomes expected from it; they are the specific goals you intend your pupils to achieve. They are not the activities that will take place during the lesson. In other words, what is to be learned is not the same as *how* it is to be learned. Objectives are not, then, what you intend to teach; rather, they are the elements you expect the pupils to master.

Objectives are most readily understood as the breakdown of aims: they are the various elements to be learned in order that the overall aim is achieved. Therefore, when planning objectives, you should do so from the point of view of what it is the pupils will have learned at the end of the lesson. This cannot be overemphasised. When we begin teaching, we easily confuse teaching with learning and presume that what pupils have 'covered' has been mastered, only to be surprised by later test results or questioning.

Objectives must be very specific. Again, an objective such as 'the pupils will learn the three stages of a river' is too vague. A better description might be 'pupils will learn and be able to demonstrate orally and by diagram the three stages of a river: upper, middle and lower', or, again, 'pupils will be able to describe and illustrate from the text the following terms: metaphor, assonance and alliteration'. In this way, the teacher is clear about what s/he expects the *pupils* to be able to do. Describing your objectives in this way shifts the emphasis from what you are doing to what the pupils are learning and this is a crucial transformation in your progress as a teacher. Research indicates that most student-teachers move from concentrating upon *their* teaching to what pupils are actually learning about halfway through teaching practice placement. This is understandable, given the time needed to get your bearings, but it is worth reflecting for a moment on the possibility that a significant amount of time and effort may have proved less than productive in the earlier part of the placement.

Objectives should be kept short and descriptive. The new teacher should get into the habit of beginning each objective with the words 'the pupils will...' This helps focus his/her attention on learning. It is best that your objectives are limited to three or four for any lesson; any more than this may lead to restricting your teaching methodology, a hurried delivery, pupil disengagement and a lack of comprehension. You should refer back to the aims of the unit to ensure that the objectives are helping pupils achieve the overall goals of the course you are teaching.

The content of the lesson

This refers to the content or material you will teach. Usually, such material is taken from a school textbook. Understandably, student-teachers tend to rely quite heavily on textbooks as they usually present the content in a well-laid-out format and provide questions, exercises and homework for pupils. There is no reason why the content of your lesson should not be based on the material in the textbook. However, you should always be aware of what the syllabus/curriculum requires. The lesson content will vary considerably depending upon the subjects you teach. What you must consider, as you prepare your lesson, is how you can best present it. This involves reflecting on the varying abilities within the group, the extent to which a selection of resources will be helpful, how best to introduce new concepts and how the various elements of a topic might best be presented as having an overall unity or coherence.

You should also consider, if appropriate, how to present the content in a manner that is attractive and, if possible, interesting to pupils. This is not as difficult as might first seem. Student-teachers, nervous of 'departing from the script' are often uneasy about trying to make content interesting. However, a little reflection goes a long way. There is no reason why you should not share your enthusiasm for the topic with pupils, elaborate on more interesting aspects, tell them about instances or applications not included in the textbook, or even in the syllabus! The relevance of the topic to everyday life should not be overlooked.

Before beginning to teach Shakespeare for the first time, it might be useful to simply chat to the group about Elizabethan life, its food, smells, entertainment and the place of public theatre. Of course, you should point out how language changes, how we use words not used even ten years ago, and that, in 500 years, school-goers will have great difficulty understanding the vocabulary we use today. You will be able to think of many other ways of doing this, but, this way, pupils become interested, or at least curious, before they even open a Shakespearean text.

Student-teachers often pitch content too high or too low for their pupils. This is partly due to the difficulty of trying to translate material covered during their degree to manageable proportions for a group of fourteen year olds.

While lessons should be challenging, it is vital that you remember that your pupils are teenagers and will have limited prior knowledge of what you will teach them. You will be surprised at the questions they ask – remember that what appears obvious to you is not to them. A good way of preparing for this is to recall your knowledge of the subject at that age. In this way, you will remember to explain new ideas, terms and vocabulary. Be careful of taking things for granted – a silent class could simply be lost rather than enchanted. Consider, therefore, what shape the content will take, how best to present it, how to compare aspects to experiences pupils can relate to and how best to ensure that they engage meaningfully with it.

It is likely that, as a student-teacher, your co-operating teacher will nominate content s/he wishes you to teach. Your preparation should be just as thorough. Sometimes, student-teachers complain that they have been asked to teach the 'boring bits' or difficult parts of the course. Remember that, one day, you will have to teach these anyway. You will not have the support of the co-operating teacher or college tutor so this is a good opportunity to prepare for what appear to be less exciting aspects of the course. Good preparation enables teachers to find ways of making seemingly dull lessons into occasions for genuinely interactive and meaningful learning experiences. There is nothing that cannot be made interesting given enthusiasm, insight and genuine commitment.

Activities comprising the lesson

The only worthwhile activity is that which encourages, enhances and ensures learning.

While lessons cannot always be totally focused on content and pupils should be given 'spaces' in which to reflect or even take a mental break, the activities you design in lesson planning should, ultimately, be directed at learning. Of course, taking a break can also enhance learning.

Activity refers to what you and your pupils will be doing during the lesson. This may vary considerably depending upon the subject. For example a Physical Education, Art or Chemistry lesson may involve considerably more physical activity than a French or Geography lesson. There are, in other words, different types of activity. Reading, for example, is often considered a passive activity, but analytical reading demands close attention and engagement. Student-teachers often record pupil activities as 'pupils will read textbook and answer questions 1, 2 and 3', or 'pupils will make notes on pages 10–14'. These are not appropriate pupil activities in that the rationale is not offered. Simply taking notes does not, necessarily, lead to learning. Student activity, be it termed 'passive' or 'active', should lead to learning.

You must consider, then, what activities are appropriate in this regard. Activities should not be organised in the hope that the pupils will not become bored, or to impress your teaching practice supervisor or co-operating teacher. Useful and enjoyable activities vary greatly, and those you employ will depend upon what and to whom you teach. When considering classroom activities, you must be convinced of their potential to enhance learning. They should be organised in such a way that they suit the pace, content and expected outcomes of the lesson. Initially, pupils may listen to instruction, move to orally answering questions, perhaps homework, so that you can ascertain learning. This may lead to pupils reading quietly, or to their peers, enabling the introduction or explanation of new vocabulary or ideas, or simply in order to progress through a chapter in a novel. Following this, pupils might undertake written work for a period, thus enabling you to invite pupils to your desk or to wander about the room to take a look at previous work or offer help. A following activity might be that pupils offer answers from the written work just completed, or move to a more advanced piece based upon it. Central to the activities is that they are directed towards learning and that they serve a specific purpose that pupils understand and work towards.

Resources

A resource is any aid that is employed to enhance pupil learning. If a resource does not do this, it is not appropriate or was incorrectly used.

Resources vary enormously and their use depends on what is being taught and to whom. Educational materials are now widely available and schools usually have a good collection, such as maps, scientific equipment, video recordings and so on. However, student-teachers should not neglect those resources that are immediately to hand, such as the blackboard or a textbook.

Teachers who plan and reflect will usually collect a body of resources. These do not need to be high tech. Magazines and newspapers are invaluable as they often deal with topics touching upon work being done in schools. Television is also very useful. Recorded programmes can be used in school or teachers can advise pupils to watch what is relevant. Often, a very simple resource works wonders. Some years ago, I observed a student-teacher teaching Geography. To illustrate how rivers deposit their load he had filled a transparent lunch box with small stones, grit, sand and water. Holding this in front of the group, he gently shook the box and the pupils were able to watch the larger objects sink and the lighter materials become deposited on top. This was an excellent and inventive use of resources and points to the importance of a teaching aid as something that assists learning; that is its only criterion.

When planning, therefore, you need to reflect on what resources will best demonstrate or shed light on what you are hoping to teach. Pupils often possess items such as drinks cartons, printed receipts or packaging that teachers of Science or Business Studies can employ. You will find that you build a body of resources that you use repeatedly and will discover what works best. Again, you will collect items of interest, while on holiday or elsewhere, to use in class. Pupils appreciate this and you should invite them to bring in their own resources that are relevant and of interest.

When using general resources, such as DVDs, acetates and so on, you should first consider whether or not they are appropriate. You must then ensure that the device actually works and is not booked by a colleague at that time. You should consider whether or not the resource can be brought to the classroom or if the pupils have to go to another room. If so, you must organise this in advance to avoid any confusion or time wasting. It is important that disruption is kept to a minimum and simply telling a group to go to an AV room where you will meet them is not advisable, as noise in the corridor can interfere with colleagues' work; nor should you overlook the temptation for pupils to take diversions on the way! The picture and sound quality of the resource should be good, and all pupils should be able to see and hear. Pupils should understand the purpose of the resource and you may decide to design a worksheet or homework to accompany it.

There should be an obvious connection between what you are teaching and the video or other resource being used. From time to time, however, it can be useful to do something purely out of interest. If there is time and the pupils are motivated, why not indulge them by showing them a documentary or film dealing with some interesting aspect of the subject ... merely for enjoyment? Don't worry too much about its immediate relevance, the pupils will enjoy being treated, will understand that it is still a learning environment, will be encouraged by your readiness to indulge them in this way and, of course, this contributes to a wider interest in your discipline.

Evaluation of learning

As the heart of teaching is concerned with pupils engaging in meaningful learning, all teachers have to know whether or not this is, in fact, happening. Evaluation takes many forms and teachers differ on its usefulness. Debates regarding the impact of state examinations, the use of grading to decide whether pupils should study at 'higher' or 'lower' levels or be grouped in streamed classes are a constant in educational discourse. While not ignoring the relevance and complexity of these issues, all teachers must engage in the evaluation of pupil learning at some stage. Some schools have strict policies and expect regular testing.

However, written tests are only one form of evaluation and we will examine other types below. In terms of lesson planning, the student teacher must consider how s/he can be certain that pupils have actually achieved the objectives set. Remembering that objectives are best worded as 'the pupil(s) will be able to...', you need to find ways of ascertaining whether or not they can do what you have planned.

There are a number of ways of doing this, but you need to strike a balance. The temptation to indulge in long periods of questioning should be avoided. Also, student teachers should remember that a good 'road map' at the beginning of the lesson and the frequent use of sparse questioning during the lesson goes a long way to ensuring comprehension.

Experienced teachers tend to develop a good sense of whether or not individuals understand what is being taught and a look or gesture will alert them to a pupil who is struggling. When we begin teaching, we do not have this 'sixth sense' and have to plan for formal evaluation. Taking for granted that you are using lower- and higher-order questioning during the lesson, you must, at the end of the lesson, check to see if the group have mastered the subject matter. Do not be too upset if they have not, you can recap at the next lesson; you may have moved too fast or too slowly, or taken prior knowledge for granted. With time, you will learn that some aspects of the course are more difficult to grasp and take more time.

Evaluating learning at the end of a lesson is challenging. Pupils are often reluctant to admit they do not understand material, particularly if the group appears to have mastered it. However, it is a good rule of thumb that if one pupil asks, you can be sure at least five others are wondering the same thing! Unorthodox as it may appear, teachers who develop good working relationships with their pupils find it easier to ascertain the level of learning. Developing a trusting relationship that is non-threatening and where pupils feel comfortable enough to admit to difficulties in the knowledge that the teacher takes this as a challenge for all, is at the core of evaluating learning. It is also important that teachers encourage an environment where questioning and the acceptance of difficulty are upheld and part of the communal experience of the group.

Traditionally, then, teachers tend to end lessons by asking if 'everybody understands'. Whole group assent does not mean you have been successful in your objectives. Some pupils *think* they understand, others want to end the lesson as soon as possible, others do not know what you have just asked and see that everybody else is nodding and others still do not understand but are too shy or embarrassed to ask. When a teacher has developed the questioning environment described above, individual pupils are much more likely to seek clarification, but you must probe for comprehension.

First invite questions. You can prompt by admitting that the subject was 'tricky' or that pupils often find it 'difficult'. Did the pupils understand how A led to B and B to C? If there is general assent and you have genuinely prompted and invited queries, then start asking higher-order questions. Ask a pupil to explain how, exactly, B led to C. If the answer is faultless, then complicate the question by introducing an unknown variable; this will reveal whether or not pupils can think their way through the problem or have simply mastered one example. If a pupil has a question, compliment it and then ask the group for responses. Dealing with questions is a difficult art; be sure to encourage pupils by telling them they are 'in the right area', 'almost there' or 'close'. Invite comment – 'Does anyone have any other ideas?' 'Would anyone like to comment?' 'Anybody see anything missing?' – in this way, learning becomes co-operative and communal. When the correct answer has been found, repeat the solution before the whole group (remembering the quiet pupils who will not ask), use the blackboard if necessary, go through it slowly and invite comment and query. Finally, ask if everybody is absolutely happy that they understand. Then, set an example of the problem for homework and announce that, if there are still pupils who are having difficulties, they can approach you for a minute after class and not to worry, as you will revise the problem again during the next lesson. This way, even the most reluctant feel confident that they have not lost out.

This is an informal and non-scientific way of evaluating learning and, like so much in good teaching, it involves establishing good working relationships with groups. They must feel that they are in a communal, non-threatening environment, where questioning is evidence of engagement. Experienced teachers develop an instinct for this; so do not be frustrated when you find that your colleagues seem to have mastered it in some magical way.

There are other ways of evaluating learning. Giving written work during or towards the end of a lesson which the pupils must read aloud, or which you check, is an effective method. You might give a very short written or oral test. However, a discussion and question session towards the end of a lesson is a valuable tool. It will highlight problems and successes and should have the effect of making you reflect on how effective the lesson was.

Homework

As with evaluation, schools and teachers differ regarding the use and abuse of homework. Most schools have a policy on this and expect teachers to assign homework on a nightly basis. There are, however, a number of factors student-teachers should consider when planning the amount and content of homework.

Most important, homework should be used as an aid to learning. This might be by providing revision of the day's material or by requiring pupils to complete exercises. It should be directed towards supporting the learning being done in class and should be carefully chosen. Avoid prescribing homework randomly. It must relate to pupil learning and, above all, must not be a 'time-filler'; pupils rightly object to randomly assigned homework and tend to focus better on work that is obviously related to what has been covered in class. Failing to really reflect on the type of homework you give represents a missed opportunity.

You should also be aware of the time constraints on pupils. Many are involved in after-school activities and others attend after-school lessons in music and so forth. Again, given that a group may have up to nine class periods per day, the amount of homework can become very time-consuming. As adults, we rarely have to continue working when we arrive home; pupils, on the other hand, are expected to do so throughout their time in school. Therefore, the homework you give should be focused, challenging and worthwhile. Why not give a series of homework assignments and allow pupils a few nights to complete it, to work at their own pace?

It is very important that homework is corrected and *seen* to be corrected *punctually*. It is very dispiriting for pupils to have to wait several days before receiving feedback. Do not return work with a large 'tick' at the bottom of the page, as if its completion is all you are interested in. You must correct it, that is, point to what is missing, give an evaluation and some encouragement. Carefully corrected homework will give you an excellent idea of how well pupils are doing and will point out any common problems, which you can then tackle in a subsequent lesson.

Finally, it can be useful to prescribe homework at the beginning of the lesson. Given that, often, the content is going to be covered during that period, it helps to focus pupils' minds, prompting them to be more attentive. Avoid shouting out homework as the bell has sounded for the end of the lesson. Some pupils may not hear you, or may claim they didn't! Prescribe homework in a calm, quiet manner, write salient details such as page numbers, etc. on the blackboard and ensure everybody understands what is expected.

Critical reflection and resolutions

Beginning teachers, in particular, are encouraged to reflect on the learning that took place during their lessons. As discussed above, there are numerous ways of ascertaining this. Student-teachers are usually required to evaluate each lesson. This is an invaluable exercise but, sometimes, the focus is on teaching activities, use of resources and whether or not the content was 'covered', rather than the extent of pupil learning. It is essential that you recognise from the beginning that a lesson in which pupils learn little or nothing is a wasted opportunity. Genuinely inspiring teaching can take place without resources, or with few books, because the teacher has successfully facilitated the pupils' engagement with the content. In short, lesson evaluation is not about your teaching, but about your pupils' learning.

Of course, these are inter-connected and you will have an intuitive sense of how well your lesson went. But the student-teacher needs a systematic and formal method of evaluation, so that s/he can discover where improvements can be made. At the most fundamental level, this will involve reflecting upon your punctuality, preparation, pacing, blackboard work and clarity. The most obvious elements around which to build your evaluation are your objectives – after all, if they were not realised, it is likely the lesson was less than successful using your own criteria for appraisal.

It is essential that you are absolutely honest and that your evaluations demonstrate meaningful engagement with the task. It is disheartening to read student-teacher evaluations such as 'the lesson went okay', 'I need to give more homework', 'the pupils could have been more attentive' and so on. These are nothing more than vague observations. Evaluation must be specific and result in concrete resolutions. Ask yourself, 'What went well and why and how can it be improved?' and 'What did not go well and how can I ensure it does next time?' These may seem rather casual questions, but they provide sensible foundations upon which to start building your evaluation.

You should be particularly aware of what went well; after all, if you can discover this, you are beginning to master the art of teaching. In speaking with student-teachers, I often ask them what aspect of the lesson was 'best' and to explain their choice. This can be difficult. Sometimes, the lesson just seems to take on a life of its own and the pupils become engaged and eager. But, upon reflection, student-teachers begin to discover that this does not happen by chance. They find, for example, that they were particularly well prepared for a lesson; enjoyed teaching the material; were not as tired; had insisted upon some disciplinary rule being respected before beginning the lesson; managed a disruptive pupil in a more effective manner; or shared a joke with the group which helped create a friendlier atmosphere. It is important that student-teachers thoroughly interrogate the lesson to discover what they did or said that led to a more satisfactory outcome. It is overwhelmingly the case that a well-prepared lesson significantly helps improve lessons on every level.

The same rigour is needed when considering what aspects of the lesson did not go so well. However, you should not dwell on this. Put mistakes that can be avoided behind you and plan for the next lesson. If being late caused disruption, plan to be punctual tomorrow. Of course, a simple resolution to leave on time may remain just that. Better to take the practical step of setting the alarm clock to ring ten minutes earlier or plan a new route to school. Decisions arising from evaluations must be practical and actionable.

If a pupil was misbehaving, then you must plan an approach that will, hopefully, prevent this occurring again during the next lesson. What this approach might be depends on you, the pupil and the school but you must, at least, try a new strategy. In this way, you begin to grow 'into' the profession.

In evaluating the lesson, you should have a list of essential questions or topics that prompt reflection and resolutions. The ones listed below are by no means exhaustive but may act as a guide:

- The lesson was well prepared and had explicit learning objectives.
- I had appropriate resource material prepared (if relevant).
- The lesson began and proceeded as I planned.
- The pupils were attentive and engaged.
- I employed a variety of learning styles and approaches.
- My instructions were clear and audible.
- Pupils participated in the lesson.
- All levels of ability were catered for in this lesson.
- I closely monitored pupils' activity, work and behaviour during the lesson.
- I was confident in my knowledge of the subject matter.
- I was punctual and orderly in the way the lesson was brought to a close.
- I gave homework/other work.
- The classroom was left 'fit for purpose' for the next teacher.

Considerations such as these should result in practical decisions, such as, 'tomorrow I will use a wider variety of teaching styles, including anecdote, illustration and examples' or 'I will walk to the back of the classroom to check that my blackboard work is legible'.

Student-teachers should not be afraid to admit when things go badly or when they feel under pressure. The most experienced teachers have difficult days; it is only when we do not learn something that these become wasteful. It is always refreshing to read evaluations where student teachers admit how difficult they found a task. Even entries such as 'I simply don't know how to get this class to behave' is an honest insight and much preferable to, 'the pupils need to behave when I am teaching them'. When the extent of the problem is admitted, you can begin planning solutions, talk to your teaching practice supervisor, co-operating or mentor teacher, your peers, the school principal and the pupils.

Honest evaluation leads to better insight, planning, teaching and learning. How worrying would it be if a beginning pilot decided not to reflect upon what caused such a bumpy landing? Evaluation is a professional and pedagogical responsibility and results in better teaching.

SAMPLE LESSON PLAN

There are countless types of lesson plan, although all should contain the same basic headings. The plan provided below is by no means the only possible type. Usually, your university or college will offer a variety of styles and you can choose which works best for you. You should, however, pay attention to the detail and evaluation in this plan.

While it is subject-specific (History) you can use it as a guide to designing your own plans. In the final evaluation, you will notice some remarks in brackets that indicate how they relate to overall good practice.

Class Plan

Topic: The Middle Ages (Introduction)

Table 3.1

Date	12-3-2009
Class	2A
Room	23
Number of pupils	26
Subject	History
Ability	Mixed
Special Needs	None

Aim of Lesson
1. To introduce the period known as the Middle Ages.
2. That pupils will begin to acquire a working knowledge of this chapter/unit.

Instructional Objectives/Learning Outcomes
1. Pupils will understand the context of the time period in question by use of time chart and oral explanation.
2. Pupils will become familiar with the meaning of the term 'medieval' by means of oral explanation and questioning exercise.
3. Pupils will understand the background to the Middle Ages in Ireland by means of text/oral explanation.
4. Pupils will understand and be able to explain the concept of hierarchy in Norman society.

Development of Lesson (Instruction and Learning)
Table 3.2

Teacher Activity	Pupil Activity
Roll call.	Same.
Collect HW, pupils take out texts.	D. Smith collects texts.
Introduction to lesson (oral explanation/ time chart).	Pupils listening with books closed.
Open book on given page.	Pupils do so.
	Pupil reads introductory paragraph.
Teacher explains and draws attention to new vocabulary.	Pupils enter new vocabulary.
Teacher prompts by using questions (e.g. 'What else happened in the Middle Ages?')	Pupils answer the prompts.
Introduction to the Normans (look ahead to Bayeux Tapestry, King Henry II, Strongbow, etc.).	Pupils listen/enter new vocabulary.
Oral explanation of concept of hierarchy.	Pupils listen and enter new vocabulary.
Select pupil to read 'The King', 'The Lords'. Clarify these, prompt by questions (e.g. 'What do you think was the role of the earl?'). (praise)	Pupils respond orally to questions.
Random questions about Knights.	Pupils respond.
Oral explanation of Knight given.	Pupils listen/follow in book.
Oral explanation of the role of 'the peasant'.	As above.
Summation of lesson by question and explanation.	Pupils answer questions/give clarification if necessary.
HW instructions (allow time to get journals, etc. and repeat HW twice!). Clear instructions, p. 46 'Questions 1, 2 and 3 for [specify date]' (be reasonable). Pupils' questions about HW.	Pupils record HW in *written* form in their *journal*.

Resources
- Text.
- Time chart.

Learning Activities
- Time chart.
- Pupil note-taking (new vocabulary and points).
- Homework.

Assessment of Learning/Instructional Objectives
- The time chart worked well, they understood quickly *where* the period was in history.
- The pupils had no difficulty understanding the term 'medieval' and most connected it with the plague.
- I had to think of more up-to-date examples of 'hierarchy' in order to explain the concept. I used that of a football team (owner, board, manager, coach, players...).

Evaluation of Own Teaching
I felt the lesson went very well although I was unprepared for some questions ('Why did Vikings have horns on their helmets?' and so on) (*need a strategy*). I was very happy with how well the time chart worked and with their interest in the Normans in particular (*a device to use again*). I felt that I might have moved a little more quickly in some places – for example, some pupils jotted down the points very quickly, then again, some were slower and I have to cater for everybody (*professional practice*).

I was happy with my voice projection, movement in the room and classroom management (*key areas addressed*). I feel that a very tightly prepared lesson such as this one means that there is little time for 'messing' (*reflecting on management issues*). I had to repeat the homework a few times as some pupils were putting away books and shuffling, etc. (*need a strategy*). Overall, however, I feel the lesson went very well (*honest*).

Implications for Next Class
I think there are two areas I should address for the next class:

1. Maybe give the homework at the beginning of the lesson – therefore they are more attentive to it (and probably to the lesson).
2. I might ask them to leave 'rogue' questions to the end (e.g. horns on helmets!). I am not sure how to address these 'red herrings' and need to devise a strategy.

PLANNING AND PREPARATION: SUMMARY

When planning lessons, the following aspects should be considered and/or included:

- Consider designing a yearly scheme of work so that you know what you are teaching and when you are teaching it.

What role does your co-operating teacher play in your preparation? Are you required to teach specific content? Are there any methodologies or resources in particular that s/he would like you to employ?

You must consider the range of abilities of your pupils and plan accordingly. Student teachers should actively seek out information on prior knowledge, test data (if available) and discuss the group with the *class* teacher.

- **Planning a lesson: Aims and Objectives**: Be clear on the difference between aims and objectives. Ensure that objectives are stated clearly and emphasise learning outcomes.
- **Transitions within a lesson**: The various parts or phases of a lesson must be considered. They should lead coherently, logically and demonstrably from one part to the next.
- **Opening and closing a lesson**: It is important to provide a 'road map' at the beginning of a lesson and to begin when pupils are settled and attentive. Lessons should conclude with questioning for comprehension.
- **Assigning homework**: Homework is an aid to learning. It should not be assigned in a random manner, should be corrected in a timely fashion and should provide useful feedback for pupils and teacher.
- **Evaluating learning**: Honest, clear-sighted self-evaluation is crucial to progress. You should ascertain what learning took place and what aspects of your teaching might be improved and how this might be achieved.

4

Classroom Teaching: A Variety of Approaches

Rose Dolan

In Chapter 3 (Preparation and Planning), the elements of a lesson plan are listed and elaborated on. One of these elements is the inclusion of activities in the lesson that will promote learning and thinking within the classroom. In this chapter, we will look at a menu of possible activities, describe how they would be implemented in a lesson, both pedagogically and procedurally, and offer a brief description of the theory that underpins each approach. As the chapter title indicates, using a variety of approaches is strongly recommended.

As you plan your lesson, and when you have decided on your aims and objectives, you need to consider two primary questions:

1. What are the best pedagogical strategies to meet these learning objectives?
2. What are the procedural strategies that will support these learning objectives?

In other words, how will I organise the learning in the classroom for the duration of this lesson? During a lesson, what will the pupils learn and what will I do to support this learning? What approach is best for learning this topic or area of the curriculum? These are some of the questions that you can ask yourself to structure yourself through the process. They are useful in the initial stages of learning to teach and will become easier as you gain fluency and familiarity with the different approaches.

DIRECT TEACHING

Direct teaching, or direct instruction as it is sometimes known, is probably the approach that is most common in teaching. It involves the exposition of the new material by the teacher, a period of practice by the pupils and an assessment of learning at the end of the lesson. Homework appropriate to the lesson is set and corrected by the following lesson.

Another way to describe the process follows a four-step model:

1. **I do, you watch**: This is the period of teacher talk, where the goals for the lesson are set out.
2. **I do, you help**: Teacher works through an example, usually on the blackboard, and checks for understanding using questioning.
3. **You do, I help**: Pupils try out a similar example under the supervision of the teacher. The teacher assesses the pupils' work to check if the goals of the lesson have been achieved.
4. **You do, I watch**: Pupils try out other examples without the direct supervision of the teacher, usually as homework. The teacher, when correcting the homework, again assesses the pupils' work.

This approach is particularly effective when you are teaching skills, rather than developing understanding.

Lessons that are mainly focused around direct teaching should begin with a clear description of the learning goals and the criteria for assessing progress towards these goals. Using WALT (what are we learning today) and WILF (what I'm looking for) is an important first step in this approach (these will be looked at in more detail in Chapter 5, pages 80–83). The approach relies on clarity of input from the teacher and a high degree of subject knowledge. One drawback lies in the passiveness that extended periods of teacher talk engender in the pupils. For second-level pupils, input lasting longer than ten to fifteen minutes is not advisable. Another concern is that skills learned in this way may not be fully understood and therefore are not transferable. When using this approach ask yourself, 'Can my pupils use what they have learned without understanding what they are doing?' If the answer is yes, then consider adding sections to the pupil activity that are specifically aimed at developing understanding.

Activities that Develop Understanding

In 1956, Benjamin Bloom described three types of learning domain. These were cognitive (knowledge), affective (attitudes) and psychomotor (physical skills). Within the cognitive domain, where most school learning is located, lie six different levels of learning. The following is a brief description of each of these levels. The first three tend to be described as lower-order thinking while levels four to six demonstrate higher-order thinking.

1. **Knowledge or recall**: At this level of learning, pupils remember the information as it was learned.
2. **Comprehension**: Pupils organise, arrange and reorder the information.
3. **Application**: The knowledge is applied to answer a problem.
4. **Analysis**: Pupils think critically and in depth in order to identify reasons, uncover evidence and reach conclusions.
5. **Synthesis**: Pupils demonstrate original and creative thinking.
6. **Evaluation**: Pupils make a criteria-based judgement and offer carefully considered opinions.

In order to develop thinking and understanding in your pupils' learning, build some higher-order thinking activities into the lesson. Design activities that require them to compare and contrast, to analyse, diagnose and evaluate, to predict, observe and explain, to represent the information in a form other than words (picture, model or diagram), or to make connections to what they already know.

Bloom's taxonomy of learning domains is also used to structure questioning in the classroom. We will look at its application in more detail in the section on using questioning as a strategy for developing pupils' higher-order thinking capacity.

The Importance of Pupils' Prior Knowledge

Having some idea of what your pupils already know about the topic that you will teach is useful when planning your lesson, particularly when you are beginning a new topic.

You can easily ascertain this at the beginning or end of a class by using a technique such as brainstorming. Write the name of the topic on the board and ask your pupils to call out what they already know about it. Equally, you might give them blank sheets of paper and ask them to do the same exercise individually. Having this information enables you to pitch the lesson at an appropriate level and to identify the misconceptions that pupils have about the topic.

It also enables you to begin the lesson with what pupils know and to build on that. If we plan a lesson that teaches something they already know, we are in what Lev Vygotsky referred to as the zone of actual development. When a pupil is in this zone, no new learning is taking place (for more on Vygotsky's theory, go to www.myread.org/scaffolding). If we teach without identifying and correcting misconceptions, the new learning is built on a very rocky foundation (for more on concepts and misconceptions in teaching, see page 71).

Explaining Clearly when Using Exposition

When pupils are asked to describe the characteristics of effective teachers, mastery of their subject is frequently mentioned. This mastery is evidenced by the teacher's ability to explain things clearly and to do so in a number of different ways. Shulman (1986) describes this as pedagogical content knowledge. It involves knowing the subject matter, knowing how to teach it, how learners learn it and how to organise the various topics so that they are learned in an appropriate developmental sequence. One of the basic errors that most student-teachers make is to concentrate on the content of the lesson without paying attention to the strategies for pupil learning. A different way of knowing the subject matter is required in order to teach it. As you prepare your exposition of the new material, it is worth applying some of the activities described earlier to the new material. Consider a number of different ways of representing the material, such as the use of metaphor, analogies, illustrations, models and examples that will enable you to explain the material fully.

When a pupil has difficulty understanding the material, re-teaching it in exactly the same way is unlikely to produce a sudden moment of inspiration. It is akin to assuming that speaking more slowly will cause your words to penetrate their minds more deeply. As you continue to develop in your teaching career, your pedagogical content knowledge deepens as you become aware of the misconceptions that are prevalent in your subject and the concepts that pupils have most difficulty with. It is worth keeping a note of these issues for yourself as they are of great assistance when you teach the topic the following year.

Questioning

Using questions in teaching is not a new idea. The Socratic questioning method as a way of teaching and developing thinking was employed in ancient Greece. At the turn of the twentieth century, de Garmo linked the skill of teaching well with the effective use of questioning.

> To question well is to teach well. In the skilful use of the question more than anything else lies the fine art of teaching; for in it we have the guide to clear and vivid ideas, and the quick spur to imagination, the stimulus to thought, the incentive to action.
>
> De Garmo (1902)

Many others since Socrates and de Garmo have written about how to use questions as a tool for learning. A number of writings in this area have looked at how questions are used in the classroom for reasons other than learning, most especially for controlling misbehaviour (Cooper 1999). Others offer some interesting information on the number and types of question used in classrooms. In the average day, a teacher asks between 300 and 400 questions. Of these, somewhere between sixty and eighty require a pupil to think in a higher-order fashion in order to answer (Cotton 1988). The remainder are either lower-order or procedural questions.

Research in classrooms has shown that increasing the number of higher-order questions to fifty per cent of the total number of questions asked has a significant effect on pupil achievement and progress (see www.highlandschools-virtualib.org.uk/ltt/inclusive_enjoyable/questioning.htm).

This section looks at questioning under two headings:

1. The types of question that we ask.
2. The strategies that work best.

Bloom's taxonomy describes six different categories of thinking and each of these can be translated into question types. Questions can be constructed for each category using the following prompts. Write your questions, particularly higher-order questions, in advance of the lesson. This enables you to focus your learning outcomes and your strategy for assessing learning by writing questions at different levels that match the goals of the lesson.

1. **Knowledge**
   - Define
   - Recall
   - Remember
   - Who
   - What
   - Where
   - When
   - List
   - Identify
   - Recite
   - Review
   - Name
   - Reproduce
   - Recognise

2. **Comprehension**
   - Describe
   - Compare
   - Contrast
   - Rephrase
   - Put in your own words
   - Explain the main idea
3. **Application**
   - Apply
   - Classify
   - Use
   - Choose
   - Employ
   - Solve
   - Write an example
   - How many
   - Which
   - What is…
   - Show
   - Translate
   - Make
   - Illustrate
   - Teach
   - Demonstrate
4. **Analysis**
   - Identify motives or causes
   - Draw conclusions
   - Determine evidence
   - Support
   - Analyse
   - Why
   - Compare/Contrast
   - Order/Sequence
   - Summarise
   - Categorise
   - Deduce
   - Investigate
   - Justify

5. **Synthesis**
   - Predict
   - Produce
   - Write
   - Design
   - Develop
   - Synthesise
   - Construct
   - Create
   - Imagine
   - Hypothesise
   - Combine
   - Estimate
   - Invent
   - What would happen if…
   - How can we solve…
6. **Evaluation**
   - Judge
   - Argue
   - Decide
   - Evaluate
   - Assess
   - Verify
   - Rate
   - Select
   - Recommend
   - Conclude
   - Give your opinion
   - Do you agree
   - Would it be better…

Pupils can also be involved in writing questions for their classmates, using the same kind of template. This has been used in conjunction with group work as an assessment for learning strategy, which is described in more detail in Chapter 5.

One of the most effective strategies to use in conjunction with questioning is called 'wait time'. This is the length of time between asking the question and looking for an answer. In the average classroom, wait time is one second or less. If no answer is forthcoming during this one second, the teacher intervenes, usually with the answer or with a strong prompt or hint. Classroom research has shown that waiting for three seconds, if the question is a lower-order one, or longer than three seconds in the case of a higher-order question, results in better answers and increased motivation on the part of the pupils. Allowing time for the pupils to think about the question and to construct an answer increases participation rates significantly, particularly for pupils who do not normally participate and for those who may have been perceived by the teacher as slow (Cotton 1988). The most difficult part of using wait time is refraining from jumping in with the answer. Silence in a classroom, with the exception of times when pupils are engaged in written work, can be very unnerving. Slowly build up the use of wait time in your lessons, explaining to the pupils that you would like them to think about the question before putting up their hands. Eventually, discourage the use of hands up altogether.

A technique that works well with wait time, particularly when the question is a higher-order one, is the use of 'think, pair, share'. In this scenario, ask the pupils to write the answer to the question. Allow time for this. Then ask them to share their answer with the person beside them. At this point, ask for answers from the class group. As you listen to the answers, allow yourself a wait time before responding. This enables you to give feedback that is thoughtful and constructive. You can point out the strengths of an answer and encourage the pupil through further probing questions to improve on their original answer.

A final word here about feedback and praise. The judicious use of praise is important in encouraging pupils but it must be used sparingly, be sincere and credible and be directed at the pupil's response. 'That's a good answer because it highlights/mentions…' is a far better use of praise than 'good boy' or 'good girl'.

Directing and Facilitating Discussion

Planned class discussions enable pupils to use talk as a tool for learning, for expressing their ideas and checking out these ideas with their peers. The discussion may take place in small groups as part of group work or as a whole-class activity.

When you plan a class discussion, there are a few things that you should bear in mind. These include the purpose of the discussion, the physical layout of the classroom and your own role in the discussion. Ensure that pupils know both the purpose of the discussion, much in the same way as you would tell them the learning objectives of the class, and the procedure for contributing to the discussion. Do they put their hand up and wait to be called on? Can they interrupt another pupil? How do they constructively disagree with another speaker? Another key decision that you need to make relates to the physical layout of the classroom. For effective discussion, it is important that the pupils can see each other. The desks and chairs can be rearranged for a planned discussion; for a spontaneous discussion, you need to decide whether the rearrangement of the physical classroom layout will enhance or constrain the emerging discussion.

Prepare the pupils for the discussion ahead of time, perhaps by giving them something to read or a questionnaire to fill out, or by asking them to write an answer to the question for homework on the day preceding the discussion. This enables you to have an informed discussion rather than random uninformed rants!

Occasionally, spontaneous discussion about the topic happens in class. When it does, pupils are talking to each other about the subject that they are learning. It usually begins with a pupil-initiated question or in feedback from a piece of group work. In these instances, the best thing that you can do is not to inhibit the learning that is taking place and to adopt a role of facilitator of the discussion. This requires you to gently manage the discussion, ensuring that people have a chance to contribute, that the discussion is not dominated by a couple of pupils and that pupils have the opportunity to develop and express their ideas, much as you would in a planned discussion. Asking genuine questions can help the discussion to develop; however, you need to decide how much you will contribute to the discussion in terms of ideas. Classroom discussions are most effective when pupils talk to other pupils with little or no intervention from the teacher.

ACADEMIC TASKS

Direct teaching is a teacher-led learning strategy. The lesson has a high degree of input from the teacher and there is a significant amount of whole-class teaching. Academic tasks, on the other hand, proceed with little or no teacher input after the task has been set up. In these strategies, there is no exposition of new material by the teacher and much of the learning takes place through discovery.

When you use these strategies, you need to plan carefully and share the learning goals or outcomes with your pupils just as you would in a direct teaching situation. Examples of academic tasks include project work, practicals, investigations, problem solving, small-group discussions, role plays and other forms of active learning. The beginning and end of such lessons need to be planned carefully to ensure that pupils have the information that they need to carry out the task that has been set. If there are instructions to be followed, it is useful to put these on the blackboard or a projector where they can be consulted by the pupils if necessary.

Using Group Work in your Classroom

Mention group work to most people and their reaction is a negative one. Most of us have experienced poorly organised group work, perhaps dominated by a couple of individuals with results that could have been achieved by individuals in half the time and with far less fuss. But well-organised group work teaches people much more than academic knowledge. It also develops our interpersonal and intrapersonal intelligences as we learn how to work with others and, indeed, learn how we currently interact with others. These are intelligences that our pupils, our teenagers, need in order to get on in life (see the section on multiple intelligences, page 70 and the NCCA website (senior cycle section) for more information on key skills for learning).

Killen (1996) defines group work as 'any time two or more students are working together, without direct intervention by the teacher'. As this definition indicates, group work can be a small activity within a lesson or a large activity that occupies the majority of the lesson. Begin with small, short activities until your pupils have learned how to work in groups. Using pairwork that lasts for a few minutes and gradually builds up to larger groups is better than launching into group work involving six groups of five pupils, all doing different things. The latter scenario engenders feelings of loss of control that only serve to increase your stress levels.

It is helpful to ask yourself the following questions as you plan for group work.

- How can I organise the lesson so that the group is clear about its objectives?
- How will we (the pupils and I) know that the objectives have been met?
- What will I do while they are working in groups?

Begin the lesson with the establishment of the learning objectives and the criteria for assessing progress towards these objectives. Do this in the whole-class setting before the pupils disperse into groups. Ensure that the tasks are clear at the beginning. Write them on the board or have instructions printed out for groups. Pupils should know what they have to do and how long they have for the activity. They should also know the reporting procedure that will be used. Do they have to give feedback to the whole class? If so, how should this be done and who will do it?

Organise the physical space so that the pupils in each group are sitting close together facing each other. Ensure that each group has the materials they need and that they can easily talk to each other and exchange ideas. Decide the size and composition of the groups ahead of time, depending on the type of task, and the time and materials available. Groups can be made up of two, three, four or more pupils. In general, the shorter the time, the smaller the group.

When the groups are composed of two or three pupils, you may decide to form those groups based around the normal seating arrangement in the class. There are a number of different ways of constructing larger groups. You may select the groups or you may allow the pupils to select their own groups. Depending on the nature of the task, it may be necessary to have groups that know each other well. If the task involves discussion of material that is emotive, friendship groups may result in a deeper discussion. However, there are also drawbacks to such groups. In general, diverse groups tend to be more powerful than groups that are extremely uniform in thought, ability or experience. You can create your groups randomly by counting, by ability (streamed or mixed), by selecting group leaders and allowing them to select the members or by allowing them to self-select pairs and then combining the pairs into groups of four.

Ensure that the nature of the task is such that each person in the group has to contribute. A jigsaw approach, where each member of the group has a specific piece of information or a specific skill, is a very effective way of increasing participation.

Organise yourself by deciding what your role will be during group work. Will you circulate around the room? Will you join each group briefly to discuss their progress, to offer hints, to ask directive questions? Will you intervene in the group process? Under what circumstances? Part of your role is reinforcement and encouragement, monitoring for non-participation, explaining and questioning, prompting discussion, and assessing the pupils' progress with the task.

Monitor the time and ensure that the group work finishes with enough time to enable the closure of the lesson. Organise the reports back, the plenary session and some way of assessing whether the learning objectives have been met (Johnson and Johnson 1997).

DIFFERENTIATED LEARNING

When teachers have been observed in their classrooms, one of the notable features is that they tend to teach the entire class at the level of the imaginary average student, even though the class contains a range of abilities (Ireson and Hallam 2001) and requires differentiation of the material and the outcomes in order to both recognise these differences and facilitate learning in the classroom. This happens irrespective of whether the class is a mixed ability one or is streamed.

Differentiation can be defined as an approach to teaching, learning and assessment that recognises the different ways in which pupils learn. It takes their prior achievements and experiences into account and matches the teaching and assessment processes to the pupils' abilities so that each pupil can learn to the fullest extent of their capability. It adjusts the curriculum to the pupils rather than expecting pupils to modify themselves for the curriculum (Hall 2002). Classroom teachers use a variety of strategies, including group work, whole-class teaching and individual instruction, to teach aspects of the curriculum.

Assessment of pupils' prior learning about the topic, either formal or informal, is an important component of differentiated learning. The assessment is used to inform teaching rather than as a tool for sorting or streaming pupils. It operates on the principle that in order to give someone directions, it is useful to know where they are.

Your role as teacher in this scenario is to gather information about your pupils, analyse the curriculum and determine the best ways to teach the material to the pupils who are sitting in front of you. Sound familiar? It should, since it is at the heart of the teaching approaches already described in this chapter. The key point with differentiation is to recognise that not all pupils will reach all of the learning outcomes in every class and to plan for this.

A useful strategy is to plan your lesson objectives by thinking about the categories of 'must', 'should' and 'could'. It is a useful way of organising your planning as it requires you to specify the minimum learning needed for the topic (all pupils must…), the next level of difficulty (most pupils should…) and the extension activities for those pupils who are extremely able in the subject (some pupils could…).

The learning objectives in the 'must' and 'should' categories relate strongly to the syllabus; the 'could' category might extend beyond it. This is known as differentiation by task. The majority of pupils will master the basics quite quickly and then move on to the next level of learning. For those who find a concept difficult to grasp, you can re-teach it, using a different mode to explain the concept. Those who master the 'must' and 'should' levels quickly can move on to what is known as an extension activity. This level is far less teacher-dependent and much more structured by the pupil. Two examples of this type of differentiation are given below.

In an English poetry class:

- All pupils must be able to identify the themes of two poems we have studied, describe which poem they like best and why.
- Most pupils should be able to use quotations from the two poems to support their assertions about the themes and describe two similarities and two differences between the poems.
- Some pupils should be able to read an unseen poem, identify its theme and compare it to the two poems already described.

In a maths class about solving a quadratic equation:

- All pupils must be able to solve the equation using the factor system or the quadratic equation formula.
- Most pupils should be able to check that their answer is correct by substituting the solution back into the original equation.
- Some pupils could graphically represent the equation and use this as another method to check the solution.

Pupils will be at different stages of the 'must/should/could' continuum depending on the topic that they are learning. Sharing the learning outcomes and the criteria for learning enables pupils to self-assess how their learning is progressing. This strategy is not about subdividing the class into three groups on a permanent basis; it's about identifying the learning needs of pupils and providing material that enables them to learn at a pace that is appropriate for them. It reassures pupils, particularly those who are struggling with the subject, that they are making progress. Identification of the areas of difficulty in their learning, identified by themselves as much as by you, and practical advice on how to develop have been found to be as important as praise in motivating learning. It reassures pupils that they are capable of learning, particularly when it happens at their pace.

BEGINNING AND ENDING CLASSES

The beginning and ending of classes can be seen as two sides of the same coin. Both have routines or procedures that physically get the lesson started or finished. Both also have pedagogical strategies, that is the activities that you and your pupils will engage in to support the creation and development of a learning climate in your classroom.

Procedures

The conventions of entry to and exit from a classroom are generally defined by the school. In some schools, the teacher has a base classroom and the pupils move from room to room; in others, the teacher travels and the pupils remain in situ. During teaching practice, it is highly likely that you will be moving from one room to another. These are some general rules or pointers around developing good procedures for your classes.

For beginning:

- Be in the classroom before your pupils if possible. If it is not possible, be at the classroom door ahead of the bell. This saves you having to try to get to class when the rest of the school is on the move.
- Set up your tools of the trade: class register, teacher's journal, textbook, markers, pens, chalk, etc. For the next forty minutes, this is your classroom so settle in.
- Stand in a focal position as the pupils enter the classroom. You may choose to stand at the door or at the top of the room. This enables you to have a quiet word with a specific pupil if you need to; it also gives pupils an opportunity to talk quietly to you if they need to. Use these few moments to gauge the mood of the pupils as individuals. This can help you to anticipate any potential difficulties early in the class. This strategy needs to be adapted if the pupils are in the classroom before you. In that instance, allow a few minutes for them to clear away materials from the previous lesson.
- Establish a routine for beginning the class. Indicate to the pupils, orally or with an overhead or PowerPoint slide, what they should have on their desks for the lesson. This saves a lot of rooting in bags later in the class. The routine is important for pupils in junior cycle, particularly first years.
- Ensure that pupils know when to inform you about things such as forgotten class materials, including homework. A brief indication to you is sufficient. Sometimes, asking them to put their journal on your desk at the beginning of class if they don't have homework works well. This enables you to begin the class, set the pupils some work to do and then check on such matters.
- Begin the class when you have the full attention of your pupils, as mentioned in Chapter 6 on classroom management.

For ending:

- Keep an eye to the time and ensure that you have left enough time to allocate homework, to answer any questions that arise about the homework and to give pupils time to write the homework into their journals. It can be useful to write homework on the board at appropriate points during the lesson. This enables pupils to make the connection between what they are learning and what they will do during independent practice outside of class.

- Establish a signal, usually oral, that informs pupils when they are to begin putting away their materials. Sometimes you get beaten by the bell. If this is happening on a regular basis, review how much material you are teaching in a class. Rushed endings usually have a knock-on effect on the next class.

- If you finish early, use the time to review material. Plan extra material for the next class. One of a teacher's biggest difficulties is gauging the appropriate amount of material for a lesson.

Pedagogical Strategies for Beginning

Establishing a mental set for learning is described as a combination of actions and statements that you design to prepare the pupils for learning the material of the lesson. This can involve outlining the learning objectives for the lesson and the criteria for assessing learning as described in the section on assessment for learning (pages 80–83), telling a story that links to the new material, posing a problem that pupils will be able to answer at the end of the lesson, showing an image or prop that is connected to the key concept of the lesson, or brainstorming about a topic to determine what they already know about the material. These actions and statements should gain pupils' attention, create expectations, motivate them and relate to their prior knowledge (Cooper 1999).

The establishment of the mental set can be used at the beginning of a lesson but it is most beneficial when used at the beginning of a new topic, a new module or when the pupils are about to embark on a different way of learning, e.g. listening to a guest speaker or watching a DVD.

Pedagogical Strategies for Ending

If the beginning of a lesson established the mental set, the ending of a lesson consolidates the learning. Reviewing the learning objectives enables pupils to see what they have achieved during the lesson, leading to a sense of achievement. This review can be an individual one or can be a whole-class exercise. End your lessons using the following strategies.

- Summarise the lesson. This can be done by you, by the class, by an individual pupil, using the material on the board, orally or in written form.

- Ask the pupils to write about these three headings in their copies:
  - One thing they already knew at the beginning of the lesson.
  - Two things they don't understand fully or have questions about.
  - Three things they learned during the lesson.
- Praise the pupils for their good work during the lesson. Be specific in your use of praise.

These strategies require the pupils to identify what they have learned and what they do not understand and enables you to communicate your expectations to them. Learning how they learn, a process called metacognition, is an important strategy in creating independent and active learners. They are the pupils, their names are on the copies, they will eventually sit state exams. Learning is their responsibility. Assisting and supporting their learning is yours.

DECIDING WHICH APPROACH TO USE

How do you decide what approach to use in your lesson? The following information is a useful guide for you. But remember, it is just a guide. Your own developing pedagogical content knowledge and reflective capacity are the best determinants of what to do in your classroom. Your knowledge of the pupils, the subject matter and the learning outcomes are ultimately what inform the decisions that you make about the processes and strategies that will form part of your lesson.

Subject-matter knowledge can be organised into five broad categories:

- vocabulary terms and phrases
- details
- organising ideas
- skills
- processes.

All subjects are made up of these categories to greater or lesser degrees (Marzano *et al.* 2000).

Direct teaching is the most useful approach when teaching the vocabulary of your subject. Give the pupils a definition of the new words or phrases and then ensure that they have numerous opportunities to encounter and use the new words in appropriate contexts. Limit the number of words or phrases that must be learned over a given period of time. Pupils need to become very familiar with the name of the concept and the concept itself before they can use it with any degree of fluency. The same is true for teaching the details of a subject. Pupils need to come into contact with details on at least three occasions with the contact no more than two days apart in order for learning to occur at a deep level. Providing numerous clear examples is important when teaching pupils how to organise ideas. In each of these three categories, pupils remember best if, after your input, they are given the opportunity to put what they are learning into practice. This practice should draw from a number of different ways of representing the information, such as diagrams, making models, pictures, concept maps, dramatising, etc. Using these different approaches enables the senses to be engaged, which aids learning and recall.

Direct teaching is also the most common approach to teaching tactics and skills. Academic tasks can also be used. Give pupils a series of examples that require the use of different strategies and ask them to describe the strategy that is being used. Asking them to compare the different strategies will lead to discovery and a deeper learning process. Another point to consider when teaching skills and tactics is the design of a long-term strategy for mastering the skills. Our tendency is to teach a skill, give time for practice of that skill and assume that the skill has been both learned and mastered. Creating a long-term strategy and sharing this with your pupils will enable them to continue the process of mastering the new skill or tactic.

Learning the complex processes of a subject requires a significant amount of guidance from you as teacher. Giving an overview of the process, maybe in diagrammatic form or as a flow chart, and indicating where it fits into the subject helps to orient the learning for your pupils. Plan activities that enable pupils to use the process but with specific emphasis on the development of a particular component. The best example of this relates to your own process of learning to teach. There are many elements that make up a lesson; choosing to focus on developing your questioning skills during a lesson is an example of development within the process. A couple of weeks later, you will choose another element of the lesson to work on, knowing that your ultimate aim is to use these in combination in the process of learning and teaching in your classroom.

There are other things that you teach in your classroom, apart from subject matter knowledge. You teach pupils how to learn, how to work with others, how to participate, how to analyse and how to evaluate. These lessons are learned in direct teaching, in active learning strategies and in group work. Dewey (1933) described the purpose of education as the preparation of children for life rather than the transmission of knowledge, instilling in them the skills of leadership, co-operation, responsibility and human relations.

CHANGING PERSPECTIVES ON TEACHING AND LEARNING

The title of this section has a dual meaning. It refers to the changes that have occurred in the international debate about teaching and learning over the past three decades and also to the change in perspective that you, as a student-teacher, undergo over the course of your initial teacher education programme.

We begin by looking at the most common perspectives on teaching and learning as described by Nolan and Francis (1992). These were derived by analysing the actions of teachers in schools rather than their espoused beliefs. The following five points represent the most common perspectives:

- Learning is a process of accumulating bits of information and isolated skills.
- The teacher's primary responsibility is to transfer his/her knowledge directly to students.
- Changing student behaviour is the teacher's primary goal.
- The process of learning and teaching focuses primarily on the interactions between the teacher and individual students.
- Thinking and learning skills are viewed as transferable across all content areas.

This enables us to make some interesting predictions about what teachers do within classrooms and how they spend their time. It also points to a strong focus on the teacher at the centre of the classroom, an emphasis on behaviour, on memorisation and the assumption that pupils are generally good learners or not, irrespective of the subject matter.

These perspectives also point to a predominantly didactic method of teaching in the classroom that is used irrespective of other, more appropriate, methods of teaching or, alternatively, of fostering learning.

International research in the past three decades has shown us that there are other ways of understanding learning, and that these ways require a different set of skills from the teacher.

These changing perspectives, arising from the work of people such as Vygotsky (constructivism and concepts), Gardner (multiple intelligences), etc., lead us to look at teaching and learning in a new way.

- All learning, except for simple rote memorisation, requires the learner to actively construct meaning.

- Pupils' prior knowledge and thoughts about a topic or concept before instruction exert a tremendous influence on what they learn during instruction.
- The teacher's primary goal is to generate a change in the learner's cognitive structure or way of viewing and organising the world.
- Because learning is a process of active construction by the learner, the teacher cannot do the work of the learning.
- Learning in co-operation with others is an important source of motivation, support, modelling and coaching.
- Content-specific learning and thinking strategies play a much more important role in learning than was recognised prior to the mid-1980s.

(Nolan and Francis 1992)

THE NEED FOR VARIETY: A LOOK AT MULTIPLE INTELLIGENCES THEORY

In 1983, Howard Gardner wrote *Frames of Mind*. In it, he expounded a theory of intelligence that was different from the view of intelligence commonly understood and measured by IQ tests. Gardner postulated that it is not simply a matter of saying whether someone is intelligent or not, it is about describing how they are intelligent. Gardner defined intelligence as 'an ability to solve problems or to create products that are valued within one or more cultural settings'. There are currently eight intelligences named and defined by this theory:

- linguistic
- logical (mathematical)
- spatial
- kinesthetic
- musical
- interpersonal
- intrapersonal
- naturalistic.

Gardner's theory has implications for teaching in the classroom. If the view of intelligence, as defined by routine intelligence tests, is a basis for classroom teaching, then concepts tend to be both explained and assessed using linguistic and logical/mathematical intelligences. For those who are intelligent in other ways, the information is not accessed easily. In addition, some intelligences, such as interpersonal and intrapersonal, may not have the opportunity to be developed in the classroom. Furthermore, thinking about multiple intelligences when planning a lesson prompts the teacher to vary the stimuli within the classroom, which in itself leads to better engagement from the pupils.

CONCEPTS IN OUR TEACHING SUBJECTS

It is Monday morning and the teacher is conducting a junior Science class on the functions and role of the skeleton. Students are actively participating in the question and answer session that is conducted by the teacher.

She asks the question, 'How can we tell the difference between a male skeleton and a female skeleton?'

The first student puts up his hand. 'Miss, the pelvis is wider on a female.'

'Correct,' replies the teacher.

The second student ventures an answer. 'Women have one more rib than men.'

'No,' replies the teacher and moves on to the next student.

This classroom snapshot holds a wealth of meaning for the teacher in the classroom, not just for the teacher of Science but all who ponder on the connections that take place within the mind of the student. Sometimes, answers are just wrong. There is no ambiguity about it. The number of ribs is not an indicator of the sex of the skeleton. Asking why the pupil gave an incorrect answer is the important lesson here. When an incorrect answer is given, it is vital to probe the answer so that the pupil's meaning may be understood and the misconception corrected.

As learners, we actively try to make links between that which we already know and the new information presented to us. We connect information, sometimes erroneously, to other information already present and, from this, we construct the web of understanding that links our disparate facts together. We are actively involved in making sense of our individual worlds. And, therefore, the wrong answers and the reasons for them may be a greater learning experience than the right ones. They reveal to us the thinking that goes on in the mind of a learner. By enquiring into these wrong answers, we get the opportunity to see where these connections are made and to understand both the conceptions and misconceptions that occur in every classroom on any given day.

Consider the teacher in this scenario: actively involving the students in problem solving, posing questions that require both recall and synthesis, blindsided by a 'wrong' answer. As we rush to give the correct answer to our students, in an effort to save time, we may inadvertently short-circuit the thinking process that a learner needs to undertake in order to integrate this perhaps factual knowledge into their web of understanding. As teachers of subjects, in schools where a child may attend up to ten different classes per day, we need to remember that the language and concepts that underpin our subject may have different meanings in other classrooms. The word 'mass' in a Religion class has an entirely different meaning from its use in a Science class. The word may look the same but the concept is very different.

The word 'concept' can mean a variety of things. It can be an idea, a theme, a general statement or the elements of a discipline. However, in educational terms, the word is used to refer to the grouping of knowledge into categories. These concepts then become intellectual magnets that attract and order related thoughts and experiences (Cooper 1999).

Think of the concepts as forming a frame on which new information is hung. It is important to place the information on the correct part of the frame but also on the correct hook. Otherwise, the interconnectedness of the information that forms the web will not be made. Vygotsky (1986) tells us that: '...direct teaching of concepts is impossible and fruitless. A teacher who tries to do this usually accomplishes nothing but empty verbalisation, a parrot like repetition of words by the child, simulating a knowledge of the corresponding concepts but actually covering up a vacuum.'

Concepts that have names have attributes that define them as belonging to that concept. It is important to be clear about those attributes, what they are and whether they are essential or non-essential attributes of the concept – what is described in the literature as critical or non-critical attributes. Unless we are clear about these, we may create stereotypes and misconceptions!

As we plan lessons and develop schemes of work for our classes, it is important to consider the definitions of the concepts that we are teaching, to determine the critical and non-critical attributes and to understand the misconceptions that may arise. For example, an island is defined as a body of land completely surrounded by water. At one level, the size of the island is non-critical but the rest is critical in the definition. Yet the continent of Australia is a body of land completely surrounded by water. This begs the question about the link between continents and islands, one which it is better to have clarified before class rather than having to think on the spot, particularly in the early days of teaching.

In maths, a triangle is the conceptual notion of a three-sided figure and a right-angled triangle is a three-sided figure that contains one angle measuring 90°.

Figure 4.1

Triangle A   Triangle B

There are some pupils who refer to Triangle B as a right-angled triangle and Triangle A as a left-angled triangle, based on a misconception that the triangle is named by appearance rather than on a mathematical principle.

When pupils are asked about the characteristics of good teachers, the ability to explain something in a number of different ways is high on the list and the teacher who thinks and teaches conceptually finds this an easier task than the teacher who teaches in a factual manner. This is the difference between the view of learning as a process of accumulating bits of information and isolated skills and the influence of prior knowledge and meaning construction on the pupils' learning.

So why did the student think that women have one more rib than men?

The Religion teachers generally have little difficulty in making the connection. It's the story of Adam and Eve. God removes a rib from Adam and makes Eve from it, ergo men have one less rib. Presumably, that was the connection that led to the answer. We may never know. But asking the question, 'Why do you think that?' would enable the misconception to be explored and corrected and the web of ideas to become even more interconnected.

HELPFUL WEBLINKS FOR CLASSROOM TEACHING: A VARIETY OF APPROACHES

New Horizons for Learning
This website offers a variety of tried and tested methods for helping pupils to learn. It also gives links to other useful websites. www.newhorizons.org/strategies/front_strategies.html.

Enhance Learning with Technology
A very useful collection of links that show you how to integrate technology into your teaching. The site also contains links to resources for differentiating instruction, developing problem-solving skills, using

collaborative learning strategies, developing thinking skills, planning projects and using questioning, to mention but a few. members.shaw.ca/ priscillatheroux/index.htm.

What works in classroom instruction?

A downloadable PDF with details of instructional strategies that have, according to research in the area of learning, the greatest likelihood of positively affecting student learning. www.mcrel.org/topics/Instruction/ products/110.

ACTION (Assessment, Curriculum and Teaching Innovation on the Net)

This NCCA site focuses on developing teaching and learning using multimedia. The site is in the early stage of development and will show the features of effective teaching and learning in different settings. www.action.ncca.ie.

The NCCA has developed a key skills framework in which each key skill is broken down into essential elements and learning outcomes. The elements further describe the skill, clarifying the skills that students will develop. The learning outcomes indicate what students might show as evidence of achieving in the key skills. The key skills framework, learning outcomes and reflection sheets can be downloaded from the following link. This page also contains a link to the school network, a project where teachers in a variety of subjects have been embedding the key skills in their teaching. www.ncca.ie/eng/index.asp?docID=263.

Alternatively, go to www.ncca.ie and search for key skills.

Highland Learning and Teaching Toolkit

An excellent resource that describes different strategies for teaching and learning and the rationale for these approaches. www.highlandschools-virtualib.org.uk/ltt/strat.htm.

Co-operative Learning Strategies for Use with Groups

Includes descriptions of the jigsaw strategy, concept webs, Venn diagrams for comparison exercises and learning role cards. www.myread.org/ organisation.htm.

Resource Materials for Differentiated Instruction

This is from the University of the State of New York. www.emsc.nysed.gov/ ciai/sate/resourcesdiffinstr.pdf.

About Learning
This looks at twelve different theories including brain research, constructivism, Vygotsky and multiple intelligences. funderstanding.com/about_learning.cfm.

Multiple Intelligences
For more information about the different types of intelligence, see www.howardgardner.com/MI/mi.html and www.infed.org/thinkers/gardner.htm. For examples of how to use MI in the classroom, see www.thirteen.org/edonline/concept2class/mi/exploration_sub1.html.

Concept Mapping
Go to cmap.ihmc.us/conceptmap.html to download a concept mapping tool. It's useful for lesson planning and for helping students to make sense of the different concepts in your subject.

Understanding Concepts and Misconceptions in Maths, Science, Geography and English
Misconceptions about Maths
www.teachernet.gov.uk/teachers/issue42/primary/features/Mathsmisconceptions and www.cimt.plymouth.ac.uk/resources/help/miscon.htm.

Misconceptions in Science
www.amasci.com/miscon/opphys.html.

Concepts in Geography
www.geography.org.uk/projects/gtip/thinkpieces/concepts.

Analysing errors in English grammar
iteslj.org/Techniques/Ho_Grammar_Errors.

5

Assessment

Rose Dolan

INTRODUCTION

> Assessment is that part of the learning process where the learner and the teacher can evaluate progress or achievement in the development of a particular skill, or in the understanding of a particular area of knowledge (www.ncca.ie).

When we hear the word 'assessment', most of us immediately think of tests and the image conjured up is one of giving out a series of questions on a page for completion by those being tested. The answer sheets are collected, marked by the teacher (usually with a red pen) and then given back to the pupil, with a percentage written on the top of the page. The pupil reads the mark, compares it with his/her peers, is either happy or disappointed with the result, places it in his/her bag and promptly forgets about the test itself. The learning has now been quantified and can now be described as 'I got 58 per cent in my Geography, History, Maths, etc.' This is even more pronounced in state examinations where the pupil doesn't even have to see the exam script once it has been marked. The learning of the junior cycle or the senior cycle is captured by the phrase, 'I got __ honours and __ passes.'

This is the type of assessment that we're most familiar with, assessment where the purpose is to measure the accumulated learning of the pupil over a period of time using a standardised test. At Christmas and summer time, in staff rooms all over the country, teachers correct tests and bemoan the fact that what they have taught and what the pupils have learned frequently do not correlate. 'I taught it, they didn't learn it' is a statement often heard at these times of the year. So how can we work to ensure that our pupils are learning what we're teaching?

This chapter deals with two key types of assessment: assessment of learning, generally referred to as summative assessment; and assessment for learning, a process also known as formative assessment. It also looks at how to decide which is the more appropriate assessment strategy to use in a given situation.

It considers the different ways of assessing as an integral part of the daily class, the topic test, end of term tests and preparation of students for state examinations. It considers the ways in which pupils can learn how to assess their own learning, the purpose of feedback and the possibilities offered by comment-only marking. The application of assessment for learning in the classroom is described throughout the chapter.

THE PURPOSE OF ASSESSMENT

The National Council for Curriculum and Assessment (NCCA) defines assessment as 'that part of the learning process where the learner and the teacher can evaluate progress or achievement in the development of a particular skill, or in the understanding of a particular area of knowledge'. This assessment can be conducted in a formal or informal manner. Indeed, as we teach, we are constantly in informal assessment mode as we listen to the responses of our pupils or check their written work to determine their level of understanding of the topic. The state examinations – the Junior Certificate and the Leaving Certificate examinations – assess learning in its most formal way. Assessment is an integral part of the teaching and learning loop and, as a central component of lessons, is a vital part of lesson planning and classroom practice.

There are many reasons for assessment.

- It enables teachers to find out what pupils have learned and, therefore, to evaluate the effectiveness of their own teaching.
- It informs future planning for teachers since it indicates the pupils' areas of mastery and of difficulty within a topic and/or a subject.
- It gives pupils feedback about their level of mastery and understanding of material that they have learned and indicates areas that they need to revisit.
- It gives pupils guidance about the level of knowledge and understanding that is expected from them.

DIFFERENT WAYS TO ASSESS

Assessment generally falls into one of two types: formative or summative.

Formative Assessment

Formative assessment records learning in progress rather than completed learning. It is an ongoing part of classroom activity and provides information for the teacher's future planning. Assessment for learning is an extension of formative assessment that aims to provide information to the teacher and the pupils about the pupils' learning and how achievement can be improved and developed. It relies on the teacher sharing the aims of learning with the pupils and uses a two-way feedback process to develop and deepen learning and understanding.

Summative Assessment

Summative assessment records and describes completed learning. It usually takes place at the end of a topic, a term, a year or a programme such as the Junior Certificate or Leaving Certificate. Summative assessments, particularly in programmes such as the Junior Certificate Schools Programme (JCSP) or the Leaving Certificate Applied Programme (LCAP), may also be compiled using information from formative assessment and from formal tests taken over the duration of the programme of study. Summative assessment is also known as assessment of learning.

Formative or summative assessments are not opposing or contradictory practices (see www.ncca.ie). Both have an important role to play in the development of learning and teaching in the classroom and beyond.

There is a third concept in assessment, described as 'assessment as learning'. This metacognitive approach enables learners to become aware of how they learn. In this part of the cycle of assessment, pupils and teachers 'set learning goals, share learning intentions and success criteria and evaluate their learning through dialogue and self and peer assessment' (see www.ltscotland.org.uk/assess/about/index.asp for further information). As pupils become more aware of how they learn, they take more responsibility for their learning and become more participative in the learning process.

ASSESSMENT STRATEGIES

Having planned activities that will provide opportunities for learning, you need to assess the degree of learning that has actually occurred before moving pupils on to the next stage in their understanding. There are a variety of strategies you can use to assess pupils' learning, from the formal test to the incidental observations in a classroom. Some of the more usual assessment strategies are listed below:

- tests
- essays
- homework
- class questions
- observation
- presentations
- portfolios
- projects or posters
- formal state examinations.

PLANNING FOR ASSESSMENT

So you've decided to give a test to the pupils at the end of the week. You want to find out whether or not they have learned what you have been teaching. But assessment doesn't only take place in the formal testing situation. As a teacher, you constantly gather information about what your pupils are learning and use this to adapt your lesson plan as the lesson progresses. It is important that what they have learned is checked out on a daily basis as well as at the end of a topic or module.

There are three questions relating to assessment that you should ask yourself when planning any lesson:

1. What will my pupils learn during today's class?
2. How will they show what they have learned by the end of the class?
3. How will the homework consolidate and extend this learning?

Correcting homework is one way to determine whether a pupil understands the material they have been taught in class. But there is a need for informal assessment of learning during the lesson to ensure that areas of difficulty are addressed as quickly as possible and that the homework is not only appropriate but achievable by the pupil. Constant assessment of learning is an integral part of any class and a key part of lesson planning is to decide how this learning is assessed on an ongoing basis.

The use of class questions is one way of assessing learning. Crafting a series of questions designed to elicit the pupils' level of understanding is a standard part of any lesson. The questions should range from simple recall to application and synthesis (see the section on questioning in Chapter 4, pages 55–59). These questions can be answered orally or in written form. The answers to these questions enable you to adjust your teaching in order to address the areas of misunderstanding and of conceptual difficulty.

Setting and correcting homework is another place where the daily assessment of learning takes place. There are different ways in which homework can be corrected. For some topics within subjects, particularly where the questions have been of the lower-order, closed variety, the work may be corrected orally during class, with copies taken up at regular intervals as a checking mechanism. When the questions are higher-order and open, with the possibility of multiple correct answers, some oral correction followed by the collection of copies for individual correction is a more beneficial process.

The concept of assessment for learning will be dealt with in more detail in the next section. At this point, reference needs to be made to the idea of comment-only marking when correcting copies. The temptation when correcting is to give a grade or a mark; indeed most pupils prefer to be given a quantified assessment of their learning. The difficulty that arises here is that the mark or the grade becomes an end in itself and the learning potential of the assessment is lost. Briefly commenting on the strengths and weaknesses of the answer, with recommendations for improvement, enables a deeper learning to take place, not just a deeper knowledge of the subject but also an understanding of the process of learning, a development of metacognition as it were.

ASSESSMENT FOR LEARNING

As mentioned in the previous section, assessment for learning is a formative assessment process that is carried out in classrooms on a daily basis. It has three main dimensions:

1. Setting and sharing the learning intentions for a class.
2. Sharing the criteria for success.
3. Providing feedback that:
   a) redefines the goal.
   b) gives evidence about the present position.
   c) provides some understanding of a way to close the gap between a and b.

(Black and Wiliam 2003)

In an assessment for learning model, the teacher's role is to set the learning intentions, to define the criteria for success and to provide feedback. The responsibility of the pupil lies in perceiving the gap between what she/he should know and taking action to close the gap (Young 2005).

So what would a 'learning for assessment' class look like? What kind of activities would take place within it?

First, classes would begin with a clear statement of the learning outcomes for the pupils, indicating what they will be learning and what they will be able to do by the end of the class. This gives the pupils a road map for the class and an understanding of what the criteria for success are.

As the classes progress, clear feedback is given to pupils that indicates what they are doing well, where the gaps or errors are and how to take steps to correct these. Sometimes this feedback is individual and at other times it is given to the whole class. As the pupils become more used to the process, they are able to self-assess using the criteria for success to assess their own work. In order to be able to do this, clear rubrics need to be developed that indicate the criteria for success in a particular learning activity. These are used to give the pupils explicit guidelines about teacher expectations. A sample rubric is given later in the chapter (see page 87).

A number of teachers who were part of the Teaching and Learning for the 21st Century (TL21) research project in the Education Department of NUIM used assessment for learning strategies in their classrooms (see www.nuim.ie/TL21 for a more detailed account of the project). The following section describes the ways in which they implemented these strategies.

1. **Specifying learning intentions and criteria**

    Begin the class with the main learning goals for the day and the criteria for assessing progress towards those goals. These are known as WALT (what are we learning today) and WILF (what I'm looking for). When a pupil is familiar with these goals, it enables them to close the learning gap between what they know, understand and can do at the beginning of a class and at the end of that class. Pupils need to know WALT and WILF if they are to learn (Baker 2006).

2. **Using questions to enhance learning**

    While closed questions are useful at the beginning and end of a lesson for a recap of material, using open questions during the class develops pupil thinking. Plan more open questions for your classes that use the full range of Bloom's taxonomy. Chapter 4 describes the use of wait time in questioning to enable pupils time to think and this should be employed rather than a 'hands up' approach. Instead, techniques such as 'think, pair, share' can be employed. In this technique, each pupil thinks of an answer to the question, shares the answer with another pupil (pair) and then with a small group.

Another technique involves pupil-generated questions. Each pupil comes up with a question about something they do not know or understand about the topic. This question is contributed to a small group. The group selects one question from their list, reads it aloud and passes it on to the next group. The process continues until all groups have a question to answer that has been generated by their classmates. The groups are then given a set amount of time to discuss the question, answer it and give the answer back to the class.

3. **Promoting group work, peer learning and autonomous learning:**
   The use of group work in classrooms has already been described in Chapter 4 (see pages 61–62). Group-work strategies that promote assessment for learning include the co-operative completion of written assignments in class, composing short dialogues, devising questions as described in point 2 above, peer assessment, completing portfolios, carrying out experiments and working to solve problems set by the teacher.

4. **Cultivating self-assessment and peer assessment by pupils:**
   Peer assessment and self-assessment are the natural progression in the process and can be introduced when the pupils have some familiarity with the criteria for learning as set out in WALT and WILF. Encouraging pupils to mark their own work and the work of others leads to a better understanding of where they have made mistakes and how to correct these mistakes. When pupils mark their own work in a group, the debate about the correct answer is a better process for learning than work that is independently marked by a teacher since the quality of thinking required from pupils is far superior (Baker 2006).

   Teachers also used two modified forms of self-assessment. These are known as 'traffic lights' and 'predict, observe, explain (POE)'.

   In traffic lights, pupils use green, amber and red cards or stickers to indicate things that they don't understand (red), that they understand to some degree (amber) and that they understand fully (green). The teacher then focuses on re-teaching or explaining the red and amber points. Pupils benefit from analysing their own learning, particularly identifying areas of difficulty for themselves.

   POE is a strategy used in Science, although it could be used in other subjects, to predict the outcome of an experiment or demonstration. Pupils predict what will happen, observe the experiment and then explain the congruence or dissonance between their prediction and what actually happened. Carrying out the process in groups is even more beneficial than working solely as individuals.

5. **Strengthening the role of comment and feedback to improve pupils' learning:**

   When pupils are given marks and comments on homework or other assessment work, the tendency is to ignore the comment and focus primarily on the mark given. The use of comment-only marking gives feedback to the pupil about the assessment but withholds the grade. Comments should focus on what the pupil is doing well, where the gaps or errors are and how to take steps to correct these. The grade is recorded by the teacher and is used to track progress and may contribute to the end of term or end of year report. When using comment-only marking, it is important to explain the rationale behind the approach to the pupils and to the parents involved.

   (Hogan *et al.* 2007)

Teachers who engage in assessment for learning tend to:

- focus on pupil learning
- articulate the learning objectives in advance of teaching
- inform pupils about learning outcomes or objectives at the very beginning of the process
- use classroom assessments to build pupils' confidence in themselves as learners
- utilise a variety of assessment strategies to appropriately assess pupils' learning
- translate classroom assessment results into descriptive feedback for pupils that indicate the strengths and omissions in the learning
- change and develop their teaching based on the assessment results.

(Stiggins 2002)

ASSESSING PUPILS USING THE CLASS TEST

The written test, completed in a fixed period of time, has generally been used as a key mechanism for assessing learning in a summative way. The comments in the earlier section about pupils learning from assessment holds true here, but the class test is also a useful diagnostic tool for the teacher. Questions that have been answered incorrectly by the vast majority of the class and common errors made in the test provide the teacher with feedback about areas that need to be taught again, using different explanations and examples.

When designing a class test, it is important to determine:

1. The purpose of the test: whether the test is concerned with factual information and its recall and/or with opinions, problem solving and other higher-order thinking skills.
2. The type and number of questions that will be asked.
3. Whether or not you expect all pupils to be able to answer all the questions in the test. This is particularly important in a mixed-ability classroom.

The starting point is to decide what the purpose of the assessment is. Sometimes, there are pieces of factual information that a pupil needs to recall – e.g. spelling, multiplication tables (although with the increasing use of calculators in classrooms at primary and post-primary, this may not be as necessary as it was previously), formulae in Maths, Business and Science, and definitions – in short, the factual information that is the foundation of a subject or that is deemed essential by the curriculum. If certain information is unavailable to a pupil in the state exams, for instance, then it is important that this information is memorised. This type of testing fits in with Bloom's taxonomy of learning domains (see Chapter 4, pages 56–58).

If, however, the purpose of the assessment is to determine a pupil's ability to apply knowledge, then certain decisions need to be made. Should the pupil be given access to the knowledge, as in an open book exam, and questions designed in such a way as to test their ability to apply the knowledge? This is particularly evident if we consider tests in Maths. If a pupil is asked to use a formula to solve a problem and s/he is unable to remember the formula, then the test initially tests memory and then the ability to apply the knowledge. A teacher correcting this test could come to an erroneous conclusion that the pupil's ability to apply the knowledge is problematic rather than his/her simple recall ability.

So as you plan the test, ask yourself:

1. What content do you want pupils to know?
2. What do you want pupils to be able to do with the content (e.g. recall, identify, analyse, synthesise, evaluate, apply)?

Constructing an Examination Paper

Having clarified the purpose of the test, you then consider what types of question best suit the purpose. As you construct a test, bear in mind that it may be made up of different types of question. This enables you to test different types of knowledge and skills in a single test.

- Objective questions, such as multiple choice, true/false, fill-in or matching, are best for testing recall of facts and discrimination between choices. They are easy to write and to correct.
- While short answer questions also test recall of facts, they are also used to test a pupil's ability to identify key concepts and state them concisely.
- Essay questions test for higher level skills, such as analysis, synthesis and evaluation, and have also been shown to affect higher level learning, since pupils study more efficiently for these types of test.
- Questions that pose problems to be solved test application of knowledge and understanding of concepts. The length of the problem to be solved needs to be considered carefully if the test is not to become one that measures endurance.
- Some subjects require performance tests where a pupil must perform a particular skill or task. Pupils need to know in advance what the criteria for assessment will be.
- Take-home exams or project work enable a richer analysis of a topic and, when used, need very clear guidelines about the word limits and whether collaboration is acceptable.

(McKeachie 1999; Cooper 2005)

At this point, begin to generate the questions.

- Look at the learning outcomes or objectives that you have designed for this topic, including the skills and knowledge that a pupil should have. Consider the content that you have taught and how it can be demonstrated.
- Decide on the assessment criteria by checking the curriculum/syllabus and ensuring that the mode of assessment and the types of question asked match the learning outcomes of the curriculum.
- Write the questions, checking them against the objectives for the topic. This helps to ensure that your questions are balanced. Consult Bloom's taxonomy for suggestions about how to word questions for different levels of thinking.
- Always complete the paper yourself before you photocopy it thirty times. This will be useful in constructing the marking scheme. Note the length of time it takes to answer the entire test. Check to ensure that you are not asking/assessing the same thing repeatedly.
- Indicate the number of marks for each question on the exam paper. This enables pupils to plan their time accordingly.
- Check your exam paper with a colleague, especially when you're new to the process. Ask them if the questions are clear and unambiguous.

Ensure that the language is at a reading age that is appropriate to the class group.
- Make sure that the layout and the instructions are easy to follow.
- Include information on the exam paper that reduces reliance on memory if you want to test their ability to use data rather than to remember it.
- Try out similar questions during class time to see where the potential areas of difficulty might lie.

How Many Questions Should I Give?

The ability level of the class needs to be taken into account when deciding how many questions should be on an examination paper. Observe the length of time it takes a pupil to do a similar question in class and use this as a rough guide. Equally, you could use the following rules of thumb, as indicated by McKeachie (1999).

- One minute per objective-type question.
- Two minutes for a short answer requiring one sentence.
- Five to ten minutes for a short answer requiring a paragraph.
- Ten minutes for a problem that would take you two minutes to answer.
- Fifteen minutes for a short, focused essay.
- Thirty minutes for an essay of more than one to two pages.

Designing Marking Schemes

The best time to design the marking scheme is when you are writing the questions for the test. This enables you to ensure that the test is doing what it is designed to do and that the marks for each question are included on the test paper. Write out the model answers for the test and look at the criteria or rubric – a scoring guide that evaluates a pupil's performance based on a full range of criteria rather than a single numerical score – that you will use to determine the quality of the answer. This is particularly important when the questions require higher-order thinking skills or do not fall into the objective question category. A sample rubric is given in the table below.

The criteria contained in the rubric do not have to carry equal weight in the marking of the test. This is something that you decide. In the example of Table 5.1, you may decide to award the majority of the marks for theme (4/10) and character traits (4/10), leaving a minority of marks (2/10) for grammar, spelling and punctuation.

Table 5.1: Analysis of a short story

Criteria/Concept	4	3	2	1
Theme of the story	The theme is clearly described and is supported with evidence from the story.	The theme is described with some limited evidence from the story.	The theme is named. There is little or no supporting evidence from the story.	There is no indication of the theme of the story.
Character traits: behaviour and appearance	Main characters are richly described. The reader has a strong image of the characters.	Main characters are described in some detail. The reader has a vague image of the characters.	The main characters are referred to by name only. The reader has no image of the characters.	None of the characters is described.
Grammar, spelling and punctuation	Few or no errors in spelling, grammar and/or punctuation.	Occasional errors in spelling, grammar and/or punctuation.	Some errors in spelling, grammar and/or punctuation.	Many errors in spelling, grammar and/or punctuation.

As you design and implement the marking scheme, there are a number of extra issues worth bearing in mind:

1. **Consequential marks:**
   If an early mistake has been made, particularly in numerical-type exams, have you allowed marks for the ensuing correct steps?
2. **Discretionary marks for the exceptions:**
   Some answers do not conform to your original ideas of good answers but have real merit.
3. **Adjustment of the marking scheme:**
   There may be a need to adjust your marking scheme as you mark the scripts. If you do this, it is necessary to keep notes of the adjustments that you have made.

MARKING EXAMINATION SCRIPTS

Since the earlier sections have looked at the test and the design of the marking scheme, this section deals more with the practicalities of marking the tests.

- Be realistic about what you can do. Put scripts into bundles and work through them. Correct for a specific length of time and take breaks. Remember that correcting is wearying work.

- Every so often, remind yourself of the significance of what you're doing, i.e. assessing a pupil's learning.
- Devise your own system for marking. Will you mark script by script or the same question on each script? Each system has its merits and drawbacks.
- Decide how you will give feedback to pupils. Will you comment on each question or at the end of the script?
- Remember to keep feedback for yourself as well. The common mistakes made in questions are indicators to you of places where re-teaching is necessary.
- Be careful of the halo effect. When you correct a really good script, it may affect the next script either positively or negatively.
- Be aware of your prejudices, especially when it comes to handwriting, tidiness, spelling, etc. Ensure that these are not unduly influencing the assessment.
- At the end, reread a select number of scripts to ensure that the marking has been consistent throughout and that the standards have remained constant.

(Race 2001)

The State Examinations Commission website (www.examinations.ie) has the examination papers and the corresponding marking schemes for the Junior Certificate and Leaving Certificate examinations. These are useful tools to guide you in designing and correcting tests. However, it is important that pupils are assessed in a number of different ways rather than just relying on the past papers of the state examinations.

KEEPING RECORDS

Recording the results of assessments is a way of keeping track of the attainment of the pupils in your class. These records should include the date of the assessment, the type of assessment given and the results of the assessment. Teachers' organisers generally have a section where the results may be recorded. You may prefer to have a folder that contains copies of the assessment/test paper, the marking scheme, the feedback sheet that you wrote for yourself and the results for individual pupils. This enables you to plan future work, to inform another teacher about the pupils' progress, to inform parents about their child's progress and to give constructive feedback to pupils about their progress over the duration of the course.

THE FEEDBACK LOOP

Providing feedback to pupils about the assessment is an important part of the learning process. Ideally, exams should be returned within five days so that the material is still fresh in the pupils' minds. Feedback can be given both specifically and generally. It is worth discussing the general results in class, indicating the areas that pupils excelled in and the areas where they had difficulties. In line with the guidelines for assessment for learning, the specific feedback, whether given orally or in written form, should indicate three areas:

1. What the student did well.
2. Where the areas for improvement are.
3. How the improvements might be made.

A UK report on secondary schools indicated that the marking of tests tended to be conscientious but failed to offer guidance on how the work could be improved, indicating that in a significant minority of cases, the marking actually reinforced underachievement by being too generous or unfocused (Black and Wiliam 1998).

STATE EXAMINATIONS

Every year, 100,000 second-level pupils sit the state examinations in the Junior Certificate and the Leaving Certificate. It would be very unlikely that you would find yourself, as a pre-service teacher, solely responsible for a class that is preparing for these examinations; however, you probably will do so in the first couple of years after you have qualified.

Preparing pupils for the state examinations involves not only teaching them the syllabus but also preparing them for the practicalities of the exams themselves. Use the resources on the State Examinations Commission website to familiarise yourself and your pupils with the structure of the examination paper, prior marking schemes used, the length of time that should be spent on each question and general strategies for answering questions on the paper.

Use books of past examination papers to give your pupils an opportunity to practise these types of question. This will also enable them to become familiar with the language of state examinations. Peer assessment and self-assessment strategies, as described in the section on assessment for learning, are particularly useful here since the rubrics for the state examinations are freely available on the website. Preparation for these examinations requires knowledge of good examination technique as well as an understanding of the topics on the syllabus.

One note of warning here: ensure that you use the syllabus for your subject as the guideline for course content rather than relying on an individual textbook. The syllabus is the official statement of the content to be taught and the learning objectives for the subject.

LEGISLATIVE REQUIREMENTS

The legislative requirements in this section are a summary of the NCCA Document Assessment in the Primary School Curriculum, Appendix C, Legislative requirements of schools in relation to assessment policy. The appendix may be accessed in full at www.ncca.biz/guidelines/appendices/appc.htm. The legislation applies to both primary and post-primary schools in the state.

There are various legislative requirements for the school in developing a school assessment policy. These are:

* The Freedom of Information Acts (1997, 2003).
* The Education Act (1998).
* The Equal Status Act (2000).
* The Education (Welfare) Act (2000).
* The Data Protection (Amendment) Act (2003).
* The Education for Persons with Special Educational Needs Act (2004).

The Education Act (1998) requires the school to 'regularly evaluate students and periodically report the results of the evaluation to the students and their parents' Part V; 22-2(b). This requires schools and teachers to develop assessment procedures, record the results of these assessments, and provide reports to students and parents about the progress and achievement of the student.

Under the Freedom of Information Acts, information held about an individual must be made available to that individual on request. Schools are not currently included under the terms of these acts. However, any assessment information or personal data recorded by the school is subject to the terms of the Data Protection (Amendment) Act.

Parents of students under the age of eighteen (and students aged eighteen and over) are entitled to access all personal data and assessment information relating to the student and they have the right to know the source of the assessment information. In addition to a student and his/her parents, the following are also entitled to access assessment information: class teacher (current or future); learning support and resource teachers; school principal; Department of Education and Science (DES) inspector;

National Educational Psychological Service (NEPS) psychologist; Education Welfare Board and its officers; and other relevant professionals.

A school's assessment policy must also state the following:

- What information is being gathered.
- Why and how the information is being gathered.
- How, where and for how long the information will be stored.

The Education Act also places a responsibility on schools to ensure that the educational needs of all students, including those with a disability or other special educational needs, are met. The Equal Status Act (2000), which promotes equality and prohibits discrimination, has implications for the forms of assessment used in schools. Assessment forms must not discriminate against pupils on the grounds of religion, age, disability or membership of an ethnic community.

The Education (Welfare) Act (2000) places a responsibility on the principal of a school to pass on information regarding the welfare of a child to other professionals involved in supporting his/her education. Information can be shared with the National Council for Special Education (NCSE), the National Education Welfare Board (NEWB), DES, NEPS and between schools if a pupil is transferring, provided that the purpose of sharing the information is to monitor and further the child's learning.

Under the Education for Persons with Special Educational Needs Act (EPSEN), a school is required to assess a pupil who is not benefiting from the school's educational programme, to determine the reasons for this and to act appropriately if the assessment establishes that the pupil has special educational needs. The principal, in consultation with the local Special Educational Needs Organiser (SENO), is responsible for preparing an appropriate education plan for the education of the child.

KEY QUESTIONS FOR ASSESSMENT

There are key questions that you should ask yourself at different stages in the assessment process.

As you plan your class:

- What will my pupils learn during today's class (objectives)?
- How will they show what they have learned by the end of the class (feedback)?
- How will the homework consolidate and extend this learning?

As you consider assessment as a tool for learning:

- Are the pupils aware of WALT and WILF for this class?
- Have you planned questions to develop thinking?
- Will the pupils have an opportunity to work in groups during this class?
- Will the pupils assess their own work or the work of others in this class?
- Does the work that they are doing merit comment-only marking?

As you design a class test:

- What is the purpose of the test?
- How long will the test last?
- What type and number of questions will be asked?
- Do I expect all pupils to be able to answer all of the questions on the test?
- What content do I want them to know?
- What do I want them to be able to do with the content (recall, identify, analyse, synthesise, evaluate, apply)?

As you write the marking scheme:

- How many marks for each question?
- Are there right/wrong answers to the questions?
- Have I allowed for consequential marks?
- Have I allowed for discretionary marks?
- Are the marking criteria clear and easy to follow?

As you correct the test:

- How will I organise the corrections?
- Will I correct paper by paper or question by question?
- Have I kept a record of the most common mistakes, etc.?
- Have I reread a selection to ensure that the marking has been consistent?
- How will feedback be given to the pupils?

HELPFUL WEBLINKS FOR ASSESSMENT

- The State Examinations Commission is responsible for the development, assessment, accreditation and certification of the second-level examinations of the Irish state: the Junior Certificate and the Leaving Certificate (www.examinations.ie).
- The National Council for Curriculum and Assessment is responsible for the development of curriculum and assessment in Ireland. The website contains excellent resources for Assessment for Learning (www.ncca.ie).
- Assessment is for Learning is a Scottish educational initiative designed to

inform teachers about three types of assessment: of learning, for learning, as learning (www.ltscotland.org.uk/assess/about/index.asp).

- Teaching and Learning for the 21st Century (TL21) is a collaborative professional development and research project between schools in the Leinster region and the Education Department of the National University of Ireland, Maynooth (www.nuim.ie/TL21).

- The School Development Planning Initiative (SDPI) was established in 1999 to stimulate and strengthen a culture of collaborative development planning in schools, with a view to promoting school improvement and effectiveness. The resources section contains some very useful checklists for using assessment for learning in the classroom (www.sdpi.ie/resources_12.html).

- EasyTestMaker is a free online test generator to help you create multiple-choice, fill-in-the-blank, matching, short answer and true/false questions for your tests. You can also insert instructions and divide your test into multiple sections (www.easytestmaker.com/default.aspx).

- Rubrics are scoring tools that list the criteria for a piece of work. They are an aid in assessment to both pupils and teachers since they enable teachers to mark work in a consistent way and help pupils to judge and revise their own work before handing in an assignment (rubistar.4teachers.org/index.php and www.teach-nology.com/web_tools/rubrics).

6

Classroom Management

Brendan Walsh

INTRODUCTION

Good classroom management lies at the heart of successful teaching and learning. It represents perhaps the most difficult challenge for student-teachers, at least in the initial stages of practice. Increasingly, indiscipline in schools has become a significant difficulty for the entire teaching profession, including very experienced teachers, and the difficulties teachers face in this area cannot be underestimated. However, some caution is required when approaching the subject.

Student-teachers tend to share stories about unruly behaviour and, as confrontations and challenges tend to cause upset and stress, these tales lead to discipline issues generally becoming exaggerated, resulting in a culture of trepidation. The vast majority of student-teachers encounter relatively few challenging pupils and find that, by and large, they quickly learn to cope with the daily run of school life. Of course, some encounter very difficult situations and while these can be daunting, they can lead to better teaching, enhanced learning, more constructive relationships with pupils and, very importantly, a deep enjoyment in teaching when properly handled.

This is what lies at the heart of discussions regarding classroom management. It is not about discipline for its own sake, it is about creating an environment in which children are free to learn and teachers are free to teach. It is about mutual respect and the creation of good working relationships. Remember, you should not expect adult behaviour from children or even adolescents. Young people's sense of humour, their way of addressing one another, their seemingly boisterous behaviour, their shared vernacular and so on are characteristics of their age group and it is important that we give them the space to simply be themselves at this period of their lives, even if, at times, we find their behaviour incomprehensible!

This does not, of course, mean that we should ignore or condone behaviour that is unacceptable. But this, too, can be problematic. Adolescence can be a difficult time, although this is perhaps increasingly exaggerated, to the detriment of teenagers, parents and teachers. Most teenagers are well balanced, reasonable, kind and willing to learn. However, when deciding upon discipline, teachers too often project their own views of what constitutes good or bad behaviour onto their pupils. Often this is subjective and based upon personal preference, drawn from their own memories of school or simply a random collection of likes and dislikes. Before deciding what behaviour we wish to encourage in our pupils, we should employ a very simple rule of thumb: good discipline is based upon mutual respect that results in agreeable and constructive human interaction, leading to the creation of an environment in which pupils can learn effectively. It is not about giving you an easier life!

While student-teachers are usually eager to discover ways of encouraging discipline in the classroom, its facilitation demands patience and thought. Usually, student-teachers will begin to voice concerns about misbehaviour within three to four weeks of beginning teaching placement and become anxious to find solutions. It is crucial, however, to understand that there are no simple answers. The causes and nature of poor behaviour depend upon a multitude of factors and there is no 'silver bullet' that will solve problems overnight. Student-teachers, therefore, are faced with the seeming dilemma of disruptive behaviour for which there does not appear to be any immediate remedy. This is usually correct, because good classroom management is based on the establishment of good working relationships, and these take time to construct. Good management is a process; it is earned through hard work, good planning, serious reflection, a willingness to learn, patience, empathy and a clear understanding of the nature and purpose of classroom teaching, that is, the facilitation of learning.

YOUR EXPECTATIONS

Student-teachers, often successful and well behaved during their own schooling, may have distorted expectations about how their pupils will behave. Having succeeded within the school system, it can be difficult to understand why others are indifferent, hostile or suspicious. Awareness of the consequences for pupils who disengage from school can cause anxiety and frustration, teachers want to see pupils succeed and become fulfilled in life. Unfortunately, they may not always convey this to their pupils. Be prepared, therefore, as you embark on your teaching placement, to encounter pupils who, for a variety of reasons, which we will look at below, do not share your view of schooling as being intrinsically good. They may have had little or no success within the system and regard it as an obstacle to be overcome in whatever way possible.

Finally, it is important to remember that successful classroom management will not happen overnight. You really will have to work hard at it, you will have to be inventive, tailor your plans and even your personality to facilitate an environment that, eventually, is accepted by all, teacher and pupils alike, as an appropriate learning space. This is not easy and it would be a disservice to suggest otherwise. Poor behaviour is a feature of schooling that haunts even the most experienced teachers; therefore, it is important that you understand its complexity and be prepared to approach it, perhaps, in new and previously unconsidered ways. Ultimately, the test is whether or not your pupils are respectful of you and one another, allowing an unhindered environment in which you can teach and they can learn.

CAUSES OF INDISCIPLINE

The reasons for poor behaviour are multiple and complex. Some have their origin in factors beyond your control and that of the school. They are anchored in wider social challenges, such as broken homes and communities, parental indifference or hostility to schooling and authority, peer pressure, and poor previous experiences of the school system. Other factors may include an unhappy relationship with the particular school, pupils within it or with members of staff. Again, a pupil may be disinterested in your discipline because of past failure, indifferent teaching, and peer or parent influence.

It is important to remember that the large group of pupils who come through the school gates each morning are a collection of individuals, each with their own histories, prejudices, expectations, aspirations and ambitions. They are not a collective of similar minds and attitudes. Each has his or her own reasons for behaving in the way they do. This is not to excuse poor behaviour but, as with any complex human action, to try to understand it. You should not expect that such a large number of individuals automatically understand, or indeed accept, your version of good behaviour. For some, your demands will seem unjust and unnecessary, certainly not insisted upon at home, or maybe even by your colleagues.

So student-teachers, before deciding on a set of 'golden rules', must give serious and sustained thought to what it is they want their pupils to achieve and to what end. Simply wanting pupils to be quiet in class is a bankrupt position unless it is based upon sound pedagogical principles, in other words, unless it assists learning.

Your Role in Facilitating Poor Behaviour!

Again, student-teachers should be sensitive to their own role in promoting poor behaviour. Certainly, lazy lesson preparation is a key factor here, as are moving the lesson too quickly or too slowly, being unreasonable, shouting in anger, failing to address pupils by their names, being offhand and unpunctual, being tardy in returning work, and being ungrateful and careless, which reveals an indifferent attitude. Pupils are quick to identify these things and generally will respond in kind. In this, they behave as any person would. In the wider world, we would consider any of these as unacceptable and our pupils are no different. Remember, you are now in a position of authority and, therefore, of responsibility: whether or not you like it, your pupils look to you for examples of adult behaviour, they expect you to rise above their occasional acts of misbehaviour and demonstrate how the adult world operates in such circumstances.

Before looking at how you might go about planning your first lesson and thinking about the rules you wish to establish, it is important to remember that a positive, friendly, reasonable attitude will work in almost every situation; pupils will not jump because you say so, nor should you want them to! The art of positive reinforcement, of showing that you genuinely care, of being deeply interested and being prepared to walk the 'extra mile' with your pupils, will do more than anything else to create an enriching, rewarding and successful working relationship.

KNOWING THE SCHOOL'S DISCIPLINE POLICY

Before deciding on the rules guiding behaviour in your classroom it is imperative that you study the school discipline policy. You must not do anything that undermines or contradicts this document. The school operates under these guidelines, the pupils and staff understand them and expect them to be followed. If you have reservations or queries, they should be directed to the appropriate member of staff. Under no circumstances should you contravene established procedures. You are a guest in the school, the pupils and staff understand and operate according to these guidelines and to attempt to subvert or work outside them is to set yourself apart from that community and to undermine it.

PREPARING YOUR FIRST LESSON

Preparing for your first lesson is a significant challenge. You feel you ought to 'lay down the rules', establish your authority and take control of the classroom. At the same time, you are anxious about seeming too harsh, you had teachers like this in school and resented it – you don't want to end up like that! You are anxious to be firm and fair, to be perceived as reasonable but businesslike, you want to be friendly but you have been advised not to be over-familiar. It is confusing. There seem to be conflicting needs.

Of course, you are probably not thinking of this group as a collection of individuals, rather as '2X' or the 'Oaks' or some such group. Again, it is possible that a staff member has told you about one or two individuals in the group to 'watch out for'. You want to make a good impression and, quite possibly, want to appear in some way different, more in tune with adolescents' concerns and interests. Of course, you have prepared the material you wish to teach, selected methodologies, revised the content, thought about those aspects the pupils may find difficult and so on. However, when planning and teaching there are three key questions you must repeatedly ask yourself:

1. What do I want the pupils to learn?
2. How can they best learn it?
3. How can I ascertain whether or not they have learned it?

It is around these principles that lessons are best designed. The danger for student-teachers is that by overemphasising possible discipline problems, they lose sight of the aim of teaching – pupil learning. Hence, the most effective way to limit indiscipline and inattention is to begin as you mean to continue, focusing on the work in hand; that is what you and they are there for and when pupils realise this, they are usually quite content to settle into your rhythm. Prolonged introductions, unnecessary time spent on detailing rules, regulations and expectations can be counterproductive. There will be time for getting to know one another as the week progresses. What is important in this first meeting is that you establish the tone, that you have confident possession of your material and of the physical classroom and that you move about freely and are thoroughly organised. It is imperative that most of this first lesson is spent in actual work and learning. You must know what this group has previously covered and what it is they are expected to know. It is useful to explain to them that you understand that last year they covered chapters 1–5, or finished the prescribed novel, and have a set of revision questions to distribute.

Being Work Orientated

A way of establishing a work-orientated tone for the very outset is to have a small test prepared. Explain that, while you understand they were not given notice of it, you simply wish to get a rough idea of what they covered before you arrived. Any group will watch a new teacher very closely. They are genuinely interested in you and your approach, and, ultimately, their expectation is that you will help them learn. They may be tempted to act up, to test your boundaries, but if the lesson is quickly directed towards work, this will become harder and although initially surprised or even resentful, pupils will usually turn their attention to the work in hand. This, after all, is what they expect in school.

Seating Arrangements

Seating arrangements play an important role in classroom management. Incoming teachers will usually find that pupils have positioned themselves with friends or in clusters. There is nothing wrong with this and a good rule of thumb is that pupils can sit where they wish on the express understanding that it does not interfere with learning and that you reserve the right to move them. In this way, a mutually understood contract exists.

Keeping the Lesson Moving and Emphasising Learning

Your first lesson should, of course, include some basic guidelines, but these should be kept simple and few. Tell the group that you will talk to them later in the week about classroom procedures, but that for the moment you want them to be, for example, punctual (specifying exactly what you mean by this) or that they must have the correct text with them for class (again, specify and explain the sanction) or that you want them to indicate their intention to ask or answer a question by raising their hand.

It is important that you pepper this first lesson with a significant number of lower- and higher-order questions. This indicates that the emphasis is upon learning. Do not simply accept 'yes' and 'no' answers, ask pupils to expand, explain, give reasons for, etc. This all helps to set an industrious tone.

It is important that you deal with any manifestations of unacceptable behaviour during this first lesson. Be confident, do not overreact and rely upon the school procedure if relevant. Use common sense. The best way of dealing with minor incidents of inattention, whispering and so on, is simply to quietly redirect the pupil's attention back to his/her work by a gesture, look or word. If you need to correct someone, do so clearly, note the name in your Teacher Journal and redirect the group's attention to the work as quickly as possible. You can have a quiet word with the pupil a moment later as you move about the room.

It is important, regardless of how nervous you are, that you maintain an attitude of calm control throughout this first lesson. There will be plenty of time later in the year to 'loosen up' and allow the climate to become more relaxed. What you are attempting to do for the first few lessons is to establish the tone of how you intend to teach. This will soften in time; the important thing is that, initially, the pupils leave the lesson knowing that your primary intention is to *teach*.

Ending your First Lesson

The first lesson should end as it began; you should ask pupils who have misbehaved to come to see you before leaving, ensure that you have noted their names and, for now, perhaps go no further. This leaves them uncertain as to your intentions and gives them something to think about. You can check with colleagues later if the pupils' behaviour was characteristic and decide on what action, if any, to take. A very useful habit is simply to direct questions at those pupils at the beginning of the next lesson. This indicates that you have taken their behaviour into account but, ultimately, being in this classroom is about learning. Finish the lesson by clearly explaining what the pupils must bring to your next lesson and give a small amount of homework. This should, of course, be related to what was done during this lesson, or help prepare for the next lesson.

Each student-teacher will approach this first lesson in a different way. Whatever your preference, it is important to keep in mind that if you do not establish a work-orientated tone from the outset, it becomes difficult to regain lost ground as the weeks progress. While increasingly unpopular with teacher educators, the old adage 'don't smile until Easter' contains a grain of truth!

ESTABLISHING GOOD RELATIONSHIPS: THE BEDROCK OF GOOD CLASSROOM MANAGEMENT

The heart of good classroom management is the establishment of good working relationships between you and your pupils. This is not always easy; relationships are complex and evolve over time. However, pupils do not expect you to be a 'best friend' to them – they have those already: what they expect is for you to form a working teacher–pupil relationship that helps them to learn. In other words, it is a professional relationship. However, you will find, when this has been firmly established, you will develop a close and friendly relationship with many of your pupils.

Some you will teach throughout their time in post-primary school and you will be sorry to say goodbye to them when they leave: watching your pupils mature and grow, both into your subject and into life, is perhaps the greatest joy in teaching. This is not gained without effort and there will be days when you will wonder if you are making any difference. Teaching is unrewarding in that we usually never know how important we were (if at all) to those we taught, or what lessons (if any) they took from us. Our goal is to enact the curriculum, to introduce and induct our pupils into a specific body of knowledge, to see them gain mastery of it, but, of necessity, this entails the creation of a strong working relationship. Such a relationship is not necessarily based on mutual liking.

In all walks of life, people work with others they find difficult and ungrateful. This is why the importance of learning as the primary objective must not be underestimated. The notion of not liking a pupil has no place in teaching because it has no place in professional relationships. Our regard is unconditional, we rise above their adolescent behaviour, we have their long-term interests at heart, remaining unchanged by the ups and downs of their behaviour because we are looking to the long term. This is central to the teaching endeavour. In a sense, we are waiting for them to catch up with us, to take their place in the adult world, and we are located close to the heart of this experience. Those of us who have taught children from entering to completing school have watched this development and have seen their behaviour moderate as they grew into young adults. By always being prepared to facilitate them, to give them room, to see the end goal, we play a formative and humbling part in this process.

There are no tricks of the trade in developing such relationships. The bankrupt notion that there are various 'skills' which we can adopt to foster good human and/or working relationships undermines the complexity both of constructing meaningful relationships and of what it is to be human. An unpopular view, but one admitted to by anyone who has spent time teaching, is that some personalities lend themselves more easily to developing good teacher–pupil relationships than others. There is a certain amount of truth in this. It is unlikely that a student-teacher who actively dislikes teenagers will have much success or satisfaction working with them. The majority of student-teachers speak about the desire to work with young people. This is not the same as wanting to teach: there are many ways one may work with adolescents. Teaching is concerned with helping young people to learn. Indeed, the extent to which graduates choose teaching as a career because they are motivated by the desire to share their subject is almost wholly neglected in studies of initial teacher education.

Creating Relationships with Challenging Pupils

An interest in your pupils will articulate itself in your everyday interactions. Sharing a joke, conversations about interests in common, lending books or music, your involvement in extracurricular activities, turning up to see them perform a play or contest a match are all everyday expressions of this. For many teachers, it is as natural as breathing to stop on a corridor and chat with a group of pupils about a football fixture or TV programme, to ask after a pupil who has been ill or simply pass the time of day. This is particularly important, however, with pupils that are challenging or disengaged. A word on the corridor can save you a lifetime of confrontation in the classroom and a reflective teacher will seize such opportunities for engagement. This is not so that his/her life necessarily becomes easier in the classroom, but because such moments present an occasion to chat with pupils in an informal context and thereby get to know them a little better.

This does not have to be about school or behaviour, in fact, it is better to avoid these topics completely. Rather, talk about something that interests the pupil. Place yourself in the role of learner, thus reversing the power dynamic. For example, if a pupil is wearing a sweatshirt that has the name of a football team on it, mentioning something about them winning or losing a recent game can spark a conversation that the pupil might never have expected. While teaching, I was in the habit of joking with pupils when their team lost, they would invariably ask me which team I supported and the mutual ribbing would lead to a few moments' conversation, this would lead to an ongoing topic for ribbing and discussion in the future, hence creating a mutual 'space' of common ground upon which to build further. Any interest can form common ground if you are prepared to work at it.

These occasions can be the perfect time to ask such a pupil to run an errand for you. This, again, may come as a surprise, as they are usually not trusted or given responsibility. This might be as simple as going to the staff room to collect copybooks, checking on something for you or collecting a key, but it demonstrates a level of trust and takes place completely away from the formal context of the classroom. Experience repeatedly shows that these minor events can result in pupils reassessing their teacher and developing a better attitude towards the subject.

It will not always work, but the few failures are worth the many successes. Some years ago, a pupil of mine covered a desk in graffiti. We had always had an excellent working relationship and I thought very highly of him. He had reached a stage in life where he was beginning to find his voice, to think politically and radically. The graffiti was the usual mix of anarchist symbols and anti-capitalist slogans. I asked him to meet me in the classroom and we discussed the problem. My point was that, while I was delighted that he was beginning to grapple with serious issues, I felt there were probably better ways of affecting the type of social change he desired than simply writing on his school desk. In other words, this was a rather weak form of protest. Why not find a political party or pressure group? This led to a long conversation about social commitment, politics and idealism. Without any prompting, the pupil offered to clean the desk and apologised profusely for having marked it. Four years later, when he was leaving school, he reminded me of the incident and confessed that this was his first introduction to thinking seriously about the issues that were preoccupying him. He had moved from the stage of pointless graffiti to developing a more sophisticated understanding of effective political action. He was deeply grateful and I was moved by his honesty.

I have elaborated on this event to demonstrate a point. The causes of actions are often an opening into an adolescent's world and can provide very real building blocks for the future, if we, as teachers, are prepared to take the time.

Managing Whole Groups

It is common in literature pertaining to classroom management to see lists of 'dos and don'ts' but these can tempt the student-teacher into believing that avoiding certain behaviours and performing others will result in a balanced, hard-working group. It is more complex than this because the teacher is involved in a constant engagement with, perhaps, thirty pupils at any one time. How then do we manage whole-group lessons?

There are several basic 'strategies' that you can develop for teaching whole groups. First, though, you and your pupils must have agreed upon a set of rules for the operation of every lesson. It is better if these are agreed on by all. They should be simple, facilitate learning, be sensible, enforceable and have consequences for those who fail to observe them. We spoke earlier about *the teacher's* subjectivity in this area – for example, insisting that pupils enter the room in silence, simply because the teacher dislikes noise, is not an explicitly pedagogically sound rule. A better rule, for example, might be that pupils indicate their willingness to answer questions by raising their hand or that they must not leave their desk unless given permission to do so.

These rules should be prominently displayed in the classroom. Once they are agreed, there can be little debate about their infringement, nor should you make a fuss, simply remind the pupil what s/he agreed to and encourage him/her to uphold their part of the agreement. A useful attitude here, as with all misbehaviour, is to remind or inform the pupils of the consequences of a prohibited behaviour. If a pupil persists you can explain that the logical conclusion is that s/he is actively seeking sanction. This usually has the effect of preventing further disturbance.

Scanning

It is important that, at all times, the teacher knows what is happening in all parts of the room. This appears daunting to student teachers, but, with time, you develop a 'sixth sense'. In the beginning, try to scan the room every few seconds. It can be useful to stop at different pupils at different times, particularly if you believe they are becoming distracted. Much is made of winning so-called 'gazing competitions' should they arise. This is a waste of time and it is by no means certain that it results in better classroom management. Humour can be the best approach here. Pupils can be reminded that they already know what you look like, that there is no time for such mutual regard, or simply told that the text is on their desk and so forth. Of course, if a pupil really wishes to 'out-gaze' you, you can invite him/her to join battle at lunchtime: this usually ends the phoney war!

Teacher Movement in the Classroom

An equally effective but better way of ensuring you know what is happening in the room is to move about. Student-teachers find this difficult. There is a psychological sense of safety – a false one – in remaining behind the teacher's desk. This can give the impression, possibly true, that you consider the other side of the desk to be their 'territory'. You must not fall into this trap. The room is your workspace.

Ensure that all bags and clutter are removed so that you are free to walk around. There is no need to formalise this, simply bring your text with you and read as you go, or allow pupils to read. If you believe a pupil is not attentive simply stand by their desk for a moment and the behaviour will usually dissipate. Again, you might pick up the pupil's copy and leaf through it, all the while keeping the lesson moving along, perhaps by having another pupil answer a question or continue reading.

Do not allow the rhythm of the lesson to be interrupted. You may choose to note a comment in the pupil's copybook. Occasionally, you may allow the pupils to work quietly while you are sitting at your desk, perhaps dealing with a single pupil. In order not to interrupt this discussion, or the general atmosphere of the group, you simply note the name and incident of a misbehaving pupil in your journal. Ensure the pupil is in no doubt as to what you are doing, but there is no need to make any comment. Again, this leaves the pupil wondering what it is you have written, does not interrupt the general atmosphere or your discussion with the pupil at your desk.

Recording Incidents of Misbehaviour

While it is necessary to keep a record of persistent misbehaviour, it is important to strike a balance and learn to use this constructively. The priority is helping pupils to learn rather than noting behaviour and sending notes home.

For small infringements, it can be useful to make the note as described above, then, as the pupil is leaving ask him/her whether or not you need to keep this incident noted. In other words, is s/he prepared to undertake not to behave like that again? When teaching, I used to refer to this as being able 'to do business'. In short, it is a trade-off: if the pupil is prepared to really make an effort, and this is demonstrated in the next few lessons, then there is no need to keep the record – in short, we can 'do business'! It is a very simple device but almost always effective. It is good to end this trade-off on a smile and words of encouragement to show that this is not about the pupil, but about the correct behaviour. It demonstrates reasonableness on your part and encourages the pupil to behave next time around. In general, try to allow a second chance. It is fair and no less than we ourselves hope for in life. Even with homework, for example, unless the pupil is a repeat offender, there is no reason for him/her not to bring the homework in on the following day, along with that night's work, of course!

Fairness, Humour and Fun

Reasonableness, fairness and empathy go a long way in dealing with adolescents. They respond wholeheartedly to these and you will find working with them more satisfactory and rewarding if you are prepared to go the 'extra mile' with them and for them. Also, it will be reciprocated. As the pupils grow to know you and to see that you care and ultimately are on 'their side', you will find that their behaviour will modify. This takes time, as with any human relationship.

Humour will go a long way in this journey. Try to gain perspective on pupils' behaviour. If aimed at you, it is directed at your persona as a teacher rather than at you personally. Also, as adolescents, their sense of fun can be childish and awkward, as they have not yet refined humour in a way that is expected in the adult world. While never accepting what should not be accepted, we also have to be prepared to share the joke. On coming across a pupil amusing a group with a perfect imitation of my teaching voice and style, I asked him if he could impersonate other staff members. He was a resounding success at the Christmas show later in the year, lauded by pupils and staff alike!

There are many ways of keeping the atmosphere light. A colleague insisted that each class begin with a joke, resulting in pupils constantly pestering friends and staff alike for 'funnies'. Another, being teased about using 'big words' in class, introduced the 'big word' competition, whereby every day any pupil could volunteer to present the longest word they had discovered. This led to new vocabulary falling into everyday use among the pupils as they strove to outdo each other with increasingly obscure and lengthy words. These little games all add to creating a tone, a culture, of fun and light-heartedness, they help create a cordial atmosphere and help make being at school fun!

Dealing with Persistent Misbehaviour

Pupils who present persistent challenges can undermine you, your work and their peers. Again, there are no simple solutions. Keeping in mind the various causes of disengagement we noted earlier, it is important that, ultimately, your right to teach and your pupils' right to learn are protected. Again, the best approach with such pupils is to attempt to build good working relationships.

You can be assured that, with work and reflection, there are very few pupils who will not respond to genuine, patient, honest attempts to help them become more fulfilled both in school and in life. With some pupils, you may be the first to show this level of concern. Previous experience may have made them distrustful and hostile but, as the adult, you have to try to see beyond this. However, you cannot allow such pupils to sabotage your lessons. You and they must establish basic rules that allow you both to operate in the same space. Of course, ultimately, you are in charge and have the support of the school and it is no harm letting them know this, but we are concerned with helping them learn, rather than just making them compliant.

Some teachers like to place unruly pupils towards the front of the classroom. This, of course, has the effect of physically identifying them as problematic and is aimed at behaviour modification rather than necessarily at learning. Preferably, an agreement that the pupil can sit where s/he likes, depending upon his/her full engagement, may be more effective. This way, the pupil is given the responsibility of choosing actions that have specific consequences; s/he has ownership over his/her behaviour. Generally, seating should be appropriate for the learning that is intended. You may want an open plan arrangement or the traditional rows of desks. Remember, if you make alterations, you must return the classroom seating to its previous arrangement out of courtesy to the incoming teacher and group.

It is important when dealing with persistently disruptive students that your concern is, and is seen to be, with their unwillingness to learn, or to facilitate learning, rather than their behaviour. We have to 'love the sinner but hate the sin'. This is not easy. Often poor behaviour appears to be directed at us personally and causes us genuine annoyance and upset. Ultimately, if the school policy allows, such pupils may be removed from your class. In all cases, a pupil who is removed should be given specific work to do and you must ensure that this is marked afterwards. They should not be allowed to use removal as an excuse for falling behind. Remember, the emphasis, always, is on learning. However, if possible, it is important to keep the pupil within the group.

FINDING SOLUTIONS TO MISBEHAVIOUR

You must reflect on possible solutions to behavioural difficulties. The only realistic solution is to find a long-term resolution and this, again, means thinking about building working relationships.

Initially, the pupil should be encouraged to realise that his/her behaviour is unacceptable. This should be done by meeting with the pupil, and a third party if necessary, to discuss the situation. The pupil should be encouraged to reflect upon his/her behaviour in terms of learning. In short, what is s/he doing that is preventing him/her or others from fully engaging with the lesson? You should have already identified the issues most urgently needing remedy so that you can encourage the pupil to consider them if s/he does not raise them. This conversation may open up unexpected areas, such as family or peer difficulties. These may need to be dealt with at a later date and by a different and qualified colleague and you should reassure the pupil that this is a priority for you. However, this meeting is about identifying a few simple rules that can be agreed upon to eliminate or lessen disruption.

It is useful to allow the pupil to suggest solutions. A good rule of thumb is to simply ask the pupil if s/he has any suggestions about how you and they might be able to proceed on a new footing. Identifying a few simple rules, such as sitting where required, being punctual or not speaking out of turn might be a useful start. Then, you and the pupil should agree on a way of monitoring this agreement. One of many ways is that, upon entering the room, you will discreetly remind the pupil, or better still, ask him/her to remind you of what you have agreed. If s/he breaks the agreement you can gently remind him/her, even by a look, of what is expected. At the end of the lesson, s/he should stop by your desk for a quick evaluation. If the behaviour has been as agreed you should congratulate him/her, without fanfare, and if appropriate, make a 'well done' note in his/her school journal. Remind the pupil, in a friendly manner, to build on today's success tomorrow and end with some words of encouragement. This process can be employed as long as necessary. If the agreed behaviour is not forthcoming, you might discuss resetting the targets so that they become more manageable, but, ultimately, the pupil must be made to understand that misbehaviour is not acceptable and, finally, will not be tolerated. This is the end to which you are both working and is the only realistic outcome.

It is important, however, that reasonable and attainable targets are agreed. This is a challenging balancing act, but habits can change in a relatively short space of time and, taking the long view, you are interested in the pupil learning to correct his/her behaviour so that learning can take place.

Keeping Records

Good record keeping is crucial. Recording instances of misbehaviour enables you to see patterns, provides a written record for the year head, principal or parents and demonstrates to the pupils and their peers that you are regularly monitoring unacceptable behaviour. Obviously, this is more effective if the pupil knows that a record is being kept. However, this is not necessary. Recording instances of misbehaviour and allowing the pupil to view it after three or four days can have a very sobering effect. You might decide that, if the behaviour is corrected immediately, you will not send the record home or bring it to the attention of the year head. A detailed record can be invaluable and a pupil can be shocked to discover that s/he has so persistently misbehaved and that you have recorded every detail. Usually, there is no need to continue recording, when s/he realises that:

- A detailed record can be made any time you wish.
- The record is accurate.
- Such a log could be sent home to parents or guardians or handed to a year head.
- The log might be permanently kept on record.

A sensible way forward is to simply ask the pupil if they agree to correct identified misbehaviour and then, take a risk; hand the record to them or tear it up. This has the effect of demonstrating that you have not kept the record simply to 'catch them out' and that you trust them. Their reaction to this is almost always one of gratitude and relief. Remind them that you may resort to keeping a new record, so it is up to them to keep their side of the agreement. This is reasonable and transparent. In almost all instances, this strategy will work. If not, begin a new log and take whatever action is necessary.

Seeking Support from Colleagues

There will be occasions when a pupil's behaviour is too challenging and you find that you are incapable of dealing with it. It is important that you recognise this and be prepared to seek support from your colleagues. This does not simply refer to situations that arise spontaneously during lessons, but also to prolonged and repeated misbehaviour that is impossible to rectify.

Student-teachers are usually unwilling to report instances of misbehaviour or seek help because, erroneously, they believe this implies that they are unable to manage their classroom. This is a serious error. First, student-teachers should be confident that their colleagues, particularly as beginning teachers, also encountered poor behaviour. Second, allowing the misbehaviour to continue is tantamount to ignoring a fire; it will not go away because you pretend it is not there. Third, and most important, failing to ensure that the pupil is effectively managed is a dereliction of duty towards him/her and your other pupils. Therefore, you must be prepared, when faced with behaviour that you have tried, and failed, to rectify, to turn to senior colleagues.

Reference to the school policy document, or simply asking around, will reveal how this operates. This is where good record keeping is invaluable.

Arrange to meet with the appropriate colleague (principal, year head, head of discipline, etc.) explain the difficulty you are encountering and outline what you have done to rectify it. If appropriate, offer some ideas around remediation and ask for help. If you feel you cannot continue with a particular pupil in your class, you should say so, and seek advice on alternatives. Some schools will simply remove the pupil and place him/her with a more experienced teacher.

Student-teachers often report feelings of anxiety about supervision of teaching practice when burdened with unruly pupils. Again, supervisors/tutors will have encountered these in their own teaching and while acting as supervisors, and should be given notice of any particularly challenging pupils and the strategies you have employed in trying to remedy the situation. Again, never be afraid to ask for guidance in this, as in any other matter: if nothing else, this demonstrates your honest willingness to learn.

KEEPING PUPILS ON-TASK

Planning for Active Learning

A key factor in good classroom management is the ability to keep pupils focused on the task in hand – learning. The most effective way of doing this is to plan lessons so that methods and activities are learning-oriented. Your task is to instruct and facilitate learning; the pupils' task is to learn. Hence, from the outset, you must plan with this in mind; learning should be the guiding principle of your lesson planning.

The atmosphere and tone of the lesson should be focused upon pupil learning and the majority of any lesson should be dedicated to this task. In other words, whole lessons given over to instruction are to be avoided. There are occasions when this is necessary, for example, in introducing new or difficult topics or ideas, but, generally, effective teaching focuses upon active learning. Student-teachers, understandably, tend to focus upon their teaching – delivery, management, tone, questioning and pacing – but often fail to ascertain whether genuine learning has occurred. So simple, concentrated, work-focused planning is the first step in creating a work-oriented lesson.

However, regardless of how well you have planned, pupils may become distracted, confused and unco-operative. Therefore, you must ensure that you follow a few simple guidelines while delivering the lesson.

Scanning

As mentioned above, teachers should at all times be aware of what is happening in the classroom. This can be difficult for student-teachers who are often over-reliant on notes and plans. But it is essential that you develop the habit of scanning the room regularly so that you have a constantly updated picture of what is happening. In this way, it becomes much easier to prevent possible disruption; not only are you keeping an eye on the group, but they can see that you are doing so. Regular scanning enables you to check who is doing what, whether they are following the work on the board or overhead projector, following the text or working on assignments set.

Target Questioning

An effective method of keeping pupils on-task and preventing misbehaviour or inattention is the use of target questioning, reading or comment. This method is made easier if the teacher has been scanning the room regularly and has identified those pupils who are inattentive or likely to become so. Direct recall or open questions aimed at these pupils before their behaviour escalates: this redirects their attention and minimises the chances of misconduct. It demonstrates to them and their peers that you are aware, not simply of what they are doing, but even of what they might do!

In all classroom management, early intervention is essential; prevention is always better than cure. As with all questioning, you do not need to restrict questions to simple recall. If the pupil cannot recall what has just been said or done, then s/he was obviously inattentive at the most basic level. If s/he does recall, then follow up with an open question; ask him/her for a more expansive response, to comment, to offer alternative solutions and so on, if s/he cannot, then s/he is either inattentive or finding the material difficult. You can ask which it is and, if necessary, recap for the pupil, or, better still, ask another pupil to do so. This way, you encourage all to remain focused as they may be in the spotlight next. This is not to catch pupils out, it is to ensure that they remain engaged and alert. This is as it should be: you are working hard and so should they.

A variation on this is to ask seemingly inattentive pupils to 'read on' from where you stop. Again, they should be able to do so. A useful way of ensuring that they are following is to let them know at the beginning of the lesson that those who fail to read when asked will be assigned extra work. You could, for example, ask the pupil to start copying out from the text. Of course, you should stop them from continuing after a few moments and light-heartedly tell them to 'pay attention' for the rest of the lesson. Using school texts as punishment is counterproductive and flies in the face of encouraging a positive attitude towards learning.

Eye Contact and Gesture

Simply making eye contact with pupils or employing body language to check or prevent possible misbehaviour is usually very effective.

We have already discussed the importance of movement in the classroom as a means of refocusing pupil attention. The benefit of eye contact and body language, as with most effective management strategies, is that they do not interrupt the flow of the lesson. Demonstrate, by looking at the pupil, that you see that s/he is not attentive and glance down at the book, or at the blackboard, etc. to redirect his/her attention. A stern look, raised eyebrow, or humorous nod or gesture should be enough.

As time passes, your pupils will get to know your gestures and will 'read' them as a correction. You may point them in the direction of the text or board, or to you, if you are the focus (for example, during a demonstration or explanation) or at whatever work is in progress. Pupils will be become accustomed to your gestures and, eventually, gestures indicating 'calm down' or 'wait' will be readily understood.

Noise Levels

Acceptable levels of noise depend upon the teacher, the nature of the lesson and the impact on colleagues in neighbouring classrooms.

Teaching is a solitary affair and we too easily forget that noisy lessons may interrupt our colleagues. It is unrealistic to expect a room containing perhaps thirty people to remain silent for the full duration of a lesson. There will, inevitably, be a certain level of noise. However, it is remarkable how work-focused lessons tend to fall into a concentrated silence. Of course, there is another type of silence ... the result of daydreaming, boredom and incomprehension.

Lessons should not begin while pupils are making a noise, settling down, taking out books and materials, and so on. This is a mistake made regularly by student-teachers. Wait for the group to settle and ensure you have their full attention before beginning. Of course, a more mischievous group may attempt to use this to delay your lesson. The solution to this is to allow a set time for settling, enforceable with some sanction for those who, quite obviously, fail to comply out of mischief. You and your pupils have a right to the time allocated to the lesson and you should, within reason, insist upon it. This can become a serious consideration when dealing with examination or senior groups, in particular. I once calculated that, because of pupils coming late from a colleague's lesson (not their fault), we would lose approximately ten lessons before the end of the year. This was not sustainable and I had to raise the issue with my colleague.

In general, noise that interferes with learning is unacceptable. However, we should be careful not to confuse excitement, enthusiasm or high spirits with malice. There are no hard and fast rules around what constitutes acceptable levels of noise. Traditionally, practical subjects tend to create noise and pupils are more often allowed to move about and chat or even listen to music. Obviously, this is not appropriate for other disciplines.

In dealing with noise levels a few guidelines should be observed.

- As a general rule, the teacher should not have to raise his/her voice for sustained periods. This simply contributes to the low-level noise in the room, is tiring for the teacher and may ultimately have an adverse effect upon his/her larynx.
- Do not shout over noise. This simply adds yet another level of noise and gives the impression that you have no other means of control. An unruly group will simply match your voice level with their own.
- In general, people do not like to be shouted at, it is rude and inconsiderate. As the adult, you are in a position, out of respect for your pupils and as an example in mature behaviour, to demonstrate alternative ways of managing unruly situations.
- As a rule, a teacher's voice should not be raised much above his/her everyday speaking level. Obviously, this will differ with everyday needs, but a calm speaking voice encourages the same concentrated attitude in pupils. It encourages them to remain quiet (where this is necessary) in order that they can clearly hear you. Remember, you may be teaching thirty-five lessons every week. You simply cannot sustain an unnaturally loud voice level indefinitely in such demanding circumstances.
- When teaching disciplines that, of necessity, generate noise, you should insist on the level being acceptable. Practical, Science and Art disciplines often entail a lot of pupil movement, collecting equipment, water, paints and so on. Pupils should understand that this is unavoidable and acceptable, but noise arising from banter, if it interferes with learning, is not.

CONCLUSION

Good classroom management is complex, challenging and necessary. This is particularly so for student-teachers. Remember, however, that almost all teachers, including those who seem to manage so effortlessly, have encountered disruptive pupils. As a student-teacher, you are not alone in facing unruly pupils; many of your peers will be encountering the same difficulties. But be assured that, with time, these difficulties become less challenging, but not without considerable effort on your part.

While employing the strategies outlined in this chapter, it is essential that student teachers realise, as early as possible, that good classroom management is inseparable from building good working relationships with pupils. This demands time, reflection, openness to change, willingness to listen, and perhaps the reassessment of long-held beliefs about adolescents, teaching, or your own values and ways of working. You will quickly notice that colleagues who appear to have few management problems have a friendly relationship with most of their pupils. They will chat with them on the corridors, share a joke, show an interest in them and their work while also being demanding and firm. Pupils respond to this because they clearly recognise, as in any human relationship, that such teachers have their interests at heart. They wish to see the pupils happy and fulfilled. Of course, developing such relationships is made easier when you like adolescents, and, certainly, teaching is less satisfying when this is not the case, although by no means ineffective or unrewarding. Ultimately, however, student-teachers need to be patient, flexible and learning-focused if they wish to succeed as good classroom managers.

SUMMARY

It is not the purpose of this chapter to provide a list of 'dos and don'ts' about discipline. Certainly, there are so-called strategies that will help, but, ultimately, each teacher develops good classroom management practices that suit the situation in which s/he operates. However, it is worth reflecting on the following issues when considering effective management:

- The causes of indiscipline can have their origin in factors that are beyond your control and influence.
- The most effective means of ensuring good classroom management is the creation of a work-oriented classroom atmosphere. This is achieved by thorough planning, regularly reminding pupils that this is the purpose of the lesson and creating regulations that are based upon this single principle.
- When preparing early lessons remember the three key questions:
  - What are the pupils to learn?
  - How can this best be facilitated?

- – How can I ascertain if it has been learned?
- There are different ways of recording misbehaviour. Experiment until you find one that works. Do not underestimate the importance of keeping records, but, remember, these are a means to an end, not an end in themselves.
- Good classroom management is aided by awareness, scanning, gesture, voice moderation, use of questioning and teacher movement.
- The establishment of a positive working environment is dependent on the development of professional relationships with your pupils. They must understand what your expectations entail and you must help them to become better learners.
- Good working relationships take time to build. Be patient, learn from setbacks and mistakes and remember that your pupils will respond to positive regard, genuine interest and a willingness to give them a second chance. Look for common ground, keep a sense of perspective, do not stand on your pride on every occasion, develop a sense of fun and always look for formal and informal opportunities to engage your pupils.
- Do not be afraid to ask for help when faced with intransigent pupils. Seek help from colleagues, talk to your teaching practice supervisor/ tutor. Remember, asking for guidance reveals a willingness to improve.
- Always follow the school guidelines regarding discipline and classroom management.
- Poor behaviour is rarely aimed at you personally: remember, you should not expect adult behaviour from children (you should, however, encourage it!).

7

Special Educational Needs

Michael Shevlin

INTRODUCTION

'Special educational needs' is a term that can evoke concern, anxiety and questions among teachers. This is hardly surprising as, until relatively recently, there was scant recognition of diversity within our education system. As a result, children who had disabilities and/or experienced difficulties in learning were often marginalised and labelled as failures. These children tended to be assigned to disability category-specific schools separate from mainstream provision. Mainstream schools, generally, did not have to take responsibility for those children who had difficulties in learning. Consequently, it was possible to ignore those children in mainstream schools who had difficulties in learning and believe that special educational provision took place elsewhere and was not required in the mainstream.

Teachers, in particular beginning teachers, are confronted with a variety of issues as they approach classroom interaction. These include planning lessons, organising classroom routines, developing appropriate teaching strategies and devising assessment techniques. Teaching a child, or children, with special educational needs may appear to be an additional imposition: however, we would maintain that developing appropriate responses for children with special educational needs approaches the heart of teaching and learning. In order to be effective, the teacher must plan lessons that enable these children to learn, devise classroom routines that include these children, use a variety of teaching strategies suited to their learning needs and develop assessment techniques that guarantee recognition of learning achieved.

In this chapter, we will explore what issues arise for teachers in developing inclusive learning environments that enable children with special educational needs to experience success in learning.

More specifically, we will examine key questions such as:

- What do we mean by 'special educational needs'?
- Who are the children with special educational needs?
- How do we foster positive expectations for learning?
- How can we enable children with special educational needs to actively participate in classroom activities and gain access to the curriculum?

CONCEPT OF SPECIAL EDUCATIONAL NEED

The concept of 'special educational need' originated in the ground-breaking Warnock Report (DES 1978) in the United Kingdom and represented a significant move away from the traditional categories of disability used in special education. The Warnock Report challenged the dominant perspectives within special education that focused on disability and separate educational provision. It clearly stated that difficulties in learning were not confined to special settings but were equally relevant within mainstream schools. In this report, it was estimated that anything up to twenty per cent of the school population could experience some type of difficulty in learning at some stage in their school career. As a result, the prevalence of these difficulties in learning strongly indicated that mainstream schools needed to address this issue urgently.

Educational provision based on category of disability was criticised as educationally inappropriate as we cannot assume that all children who have a particular disability will have the same learning needs. Also, knowing that a child has cerebral palsy or Down Syndrome tells us very little about their actual learning needs as there is a wide variation in strengths and weaknesses in learning among children who have the same disability. Thinking about special education was heavily influenced by the Warnock Report as, previous to this, special education was regarded as the preserve of special schools and specialist personnel.

The Warnock Report defined special education as consisting of 'any form of additional help, wherever it is provided ... to overcome educational difficulty' (DES 1978:para. 1.10). It was recommended that the existing categories of disability should be abolished and replaced with the generic term 'special educational needs' to refer to all pupils who, for whatever reasons, require additional educational support. It was asserted that there was a continuum of individual learning need among all pupils and that difficulty in learning was a common aspect of school life as many pupils may encounter difficulties in learning at some stage of their school careers. Beveridge (1999:para 3) commented that three dimensions of special educational need were acknowledged in the Warnock Report: '... special educational needs might be long-lasting or short-term, specific to particular aspects of learning or more general, and will also vary in the degree to which they affect a child's learning.'

For a minority of pupils the difficulties in learning will be severe enough to require substantial additional help that is extra to what is available in the ordinary classroom.

Since the publication of the Warnock Report, there have been attempts to refine the term 'special educational need' to express the interactive nature of learning difficulties. Some examples include 'individual educational need' (Hart 1996) and 'barriers to learning' (Booth 1998), and 'additional needs' has been adopted as the official designation in Scotland.

WHO ARE THE CHILDREN WITH SPECIAL EDUCATIONAL NEEDS?

Children with special educational needs form a very varied group that includes children with and without identified disabilities. Within the Irish context, the 2004 Education for Persons with Special Educational Needs Act (EPSEN) defines special educational needs as:

> 'A restriction in the capacity of the person to participate in and benefit from education on account of an enduring physical, sensory, mental health or learning disability or any other condition, which results in a person learning differently from a person without that condition.'

This definition recognises that difficulties in learning are not solely the result of within-child factors.

Within the cohort of children identified as having special educational needs, there are children who experience significant difficulties in learning and others who have less serious learning difficulties. Children experiencing significant difficulties require substantial additional support including interventions such as modified teaching approaches, specialist resources and curriculum modification. Children with less significant difficulties receive a lower level of support through a differentiated curriculum and access to learning support.

We can conclude that a child is deemed to have a 'special educational need' if s/he requires considerable additional educational provision in comparison to his/her peers. While the term 'special educational need' is commonly used in schools and DES (Department of Education and Science) documents, the DES retains a categorical approach in relation to identification, assessment and allocation of resources.

The classifications in relation to sensory and physical disability are relatively straightforward, though children with a wide variety of physical disabilities are grouped under the general title of 'physical disabilities' for educational and administrative purposes. Children with identifiable learning difficulties (formerly known as 'mentally handicapped') are designated as having 'general learning disabilities', which are further subdivided into 'mild', 'moderate' or 'severe and profound', depending on the level of difficulty experienced by the child. Children with emotional/behavioural difficulties are classified under the term 'emotional/behavioural disturbance', a medical term that can suggest a very negative picture of these children. Children who have dyslexia are classified under the umbrella term 'specific learning disabilities'. Children on the autistic spectrum are classified as having an 'autistic spectrum disorder' (ASD), a term that can have negative connotations.

In this section, a brief overview of some of the major types of difficulties in learning classified as 'special educational needs' will be provided. However, we always need to tread cautiously as within the confines of a chapter, broad indicators can be provided rather than the in-depth knowledge required for appropriate educational interventions. More detailed information on various types of special educational needs is available from www.scotens.org.

Children who have mild general learning disabilities constitute the largest group of children in mainstream schools who have special educational needs. These children have been assessed by an educational psychologist and achieved an IQ score in the range 50–70 approximately, which is considerably below average. Often there is no apparent cause of mild general learning difficulty.

The second largest group consists of children with specific learning disabilities (dyslexia) who were often in mainstream schools but experienced significant literacy difficulties (for a more detailed discussion see Task Force on Dyslexia Report 2002). Due to the lack of knowledge about the impact of dyslexia on learning, their difficulties in literacy were attributed to a lack of intelligence, lack of concentration or laziness. In the past, some educationalists have questioned the existence and validity of a diagnosis of dyslexia, though, as Ball, Hughes and McCormack (2006:para 1) observe: 'Educationalists now agree that dyslexia is a fact; while there is still some argument about the prevalence of the difficulty, nobody seriously questions its existence.'

These children are usually within the average range of intelligence; however, their basic reading, writing and mathematical skills are much lower than expected for their assessed intelligence. There is often a marked discrepancy between their oral proficiency and their written work. 'Specific learning disability' is a generic term that includes: dyslexia, a difficulty with reading, writing and spelling (the most common issue); dyscalculia, a difficulty with mathematics; dysgraphia, a difficulty with handwriting; and dyspraxia, a difficulty with motor co-ordination.

Recently, the educational needs of children with autistic spectrum disorder have been increasingly recognised through the provision of special classes in mainstream schools. Autism is a very complex condition (for fuller discussion see the Task Force on Autism Report 2001). It is generally agreed that there is a triad of impairments associated with autism, including social interaction (the child has immense difficulty in the initiation and maintenance of social contact with peers); language and communication (the child can have a literal understanding of the social aspects of language and so finds turn-taking and imaginative thinking difficult); and limited behavioural repertoire (the child will often engage in repetitive play activities and have a very narrow range of interests).

More recently, there has been increased identification of the condition ADHD (Attention Deficit Hyperactivity Disorder), which can have a major impact on the capacity of children to learn successfully and be active participants in classroom learning. Barklay (1997) observed that these children have difficulties in the 'executive functions' of the brain that centre around self-regulation skills and involve impairments in working memory (drawing on internalised information for assessing situations and for forward planning); internalised speech (rehearsing activities, appraising situations, organising events); motivational appraisal ('to think before we act', judge the emotional impact on other people and the likely outcomes of our behaviour); and reconstitution (analysing past behaviours in order to plan new and appropriate behaviours). As a result, these children have great difficulty in conforming to classroom routines, may act inappropriately and be prone to inattention and lack of concentration. School and classroom routines can be very stressful for these children.

- While some children who have a disability may have a special educational need, the teacher cannot assume automatically that a child with a disability has a special educational need. Children with disabilities may have difficulties accessing the curriculum and require adaptations to the learning environment; however, this does not mean that they should be deemed to have a special educational need. Failure to make this distinction often leads to confusion and can result in inappropriate class placement, lowered expectations and inadequate adaptations. It is relatively common for a child with a physical disability, for example, to require assistive technology (ICT software programs, for example) to enable her/him to gain access to the curriculum. Additionally, a child may need a reasonable accommodation in taking examinations in order to convey their subject knowledge effectively. It is fairly evident that these examples constitute access rather than learning needs.

Rose and Howley (2006) alert us to the danger of believing that because a child has a disability s/he automatically has a special educational need too. Teachers obviously require information about the educational implications of a particular disability, such as cerebral palsy, but they have to be very careful that 'the low expectations which are often fuelled by disabling labels can lead to under-achievement and a denial of entitlement to appropriate learning opportunities' (Rose and Howley 2006:xx). In addition, children for whom English is a second language may require intensive language support but this does not necessarily mean that they have special educational needs.

After a long struggle, it is now generally recognised that children with disabilities are a heterogeneous grouping and do not necessarily share similar characteristics. These children are as varied and disparate as the rest of their peers in the school population. Children with disabilities include those who have physical or sensory impairments, those who have a variety of identified general learning disabilities, those who have emotional and behavioural difficulties and others who have mental health problems or hidden/invisible disabilities. In the past, children with disabilities were educated separately from their peers according to a disability category (physical, sensory, general learning disabilities, and emotional and behavioural difficulties).

FAILURE TO LEARN

Consistent prolonged failure in learning is obviously very frustrating for the child and it can also affect the teacher's confidence and belief that they can make a difference in enabling the child to learn. In order to understand the complex processes involved in learning failure, teachers need to examine their beliefs about its causes.

The traditional model (deficit model) attributed learning difficulties to individual pupil deficits. These deficits included:

*   Below average intelligence.
*   Problems generalising learning to new situations.
*   Poor concentration.
*   Low self-esteem and lack of confidence.
*   Behavioural and emotional reactions to failure.

Listing these types of pupil deficits could overwhelm the teacher and lead her/him to believe that progress in learning will be almost impossible for this child.

However, the Warnock Report (1978) represented an attempt to move beyond the traditional explanations, as Beveridge (1999:4) observed:

> 'It did not deny that within-child factors can have a significant impact on learning, but the concept of special educational need which was put forward was far more concerned with the interaction between the child and the learning contexts which the child experiences.'

Educationalists have gradually come to accept that difficulties in learning arise from a combination of within-child factors and aspects of the child's learning environment: 'It allows us to view children's needs as a result of a mismatch between the knowledge, skills and experiences they bring to their learning situations and the demands that are made of them' (Beveridge 1999:4). However, the traditional within-child perspective retains a powerful hold over teacher belief systems and still influences policy decisions.

An alternative theory ('environmental demands') attributed learning failure to factors such as ineffective teaching strategies, poor classroom organisation, and an inappropriate match between task demands and learner skills/knowledge. Frederickson and Cline (2002:42) maintain that the reasons for learning difficulties are complex and probably lie in a combination of both approaches: '... the level of need as a result of a complex interaction between the child's strengths and weaknesses, the level of support available and the appropriateness of the education being provided.'

When children fail to learn despite repeated attempts by the teacher to support learning, teachers can begin to focus on what is wrong with the child. However, focusing on within-child deficits will only provide part of the answer to enabling the child to overcome their failure in learning. Creating an appropriate learning environment will involve consideration of factors outside the child such as the '... quality and type of instruction given, teacher expectations, relevance of work set, classroom environment, interpersonal dynamics within the class social group and rapport with the teacher. These factors are much more amenable to change than are factors within the child or within the family background or culture' (Westwood 1997:9).

When children fail to learn basic skills, their confidence and belief in themselves as learners is affected. As a result, the child will do anything to avoid the task and so miss out on opportunities to gain proficiency. Task avoidance can lead to further problems as the child may engage in attention-seeking behaviour, disrupt classroom work and get into confrontation situations with the teacher. The child who experiences repeated failure 'can develop the perception that achieving success in learning is completely outside their control no matter what they do' (Frederickson and Cline 2002:322). Children who have experienced repeated failure in learning at primary school may be totally disaffected with classroom learning by the time they reach secondary school.

In order to overcome the failure cycle, tasks need to be structured in a way that enables the child to achieve success. Teachers have commented that children experiencing failure in learning often adopt very ineffective approaches to the learning task. It is evident that these children have little idea how to tackle the task given, employ haphazard strategies and do not reflect on their work. As a result, they have a high failure rate in learning tasks and little motivation to stay on-task and persist. Westwood (1997:12) suggests that these pupils benefit most 'from explicit teaching of new concepts, skills and strategies'. These students need 'to be placed in well-managed classrooms, with clear, active teaching and where students spend productive time on-task, experiencing successful practice and knowing that they are reaching mastery'.

ENSHRINING KEY PRINCIPLES

Within the confines of this chapter, it will only be possible to provide a framework for thinking around special educational needs and outline key principles and important guidelines in relation to developing appropriate learning environments for children and young people with special educational needs. It is evident that responding appropriately to the learning needs of these children is a complex process that requires

itment, knowledge and positive experience. However, while the
ning teacher will not be expected to understand all the educational
implications of special educational needs, it is reasonable to expect her/him
to begin to acquire and use basic knowledge around this issue.

Key principles for all teachers in relation to children and young people
with special educational needs are outlined by O'Brien and Guiney
(2001:11–13):

- All children have a right to high quality education.
- Every child can learn.
- Every teacher is also a learner.
- Learning is a social and active process and involves mutual relationships.
- Progress for all learners will be expected, recognised and rewarded.

More specifically, implementing these principles in practice will involve:
having positive expectations and making no unwarranted assumptions
about capacity for learning; ensuring active participation in classroom
activities; and adapting teaching strategies to enable curricular access.

ASSUMPTIONS AND EXPECTATIONS

Teacher expectations have a powerful influence on pupil achievement.
These expectations for pupil learning are usually based on a set of
assumptions. These assumptions may have a solid knowledge base:
however, in the area of special educational needs, they may be based on
stereotypical, ill-informed perspectives.

This is hardly surprising as, in the past, special education was seen as
separate provision with little relevance to the mainstream teacher. As a
result, this isolation supported the development of certain myths about
children with special educational needs and particular beliefs about
appropriate teaching strategies. Children and young people with special
educational needs were perceived as qualitatively different from their peers;
their social and learning needs were substantially different from their peer
group and it was believed that they could learn very little.

Lowered expectations can limit both opportunities for and success in
learning as illustrated by a pupil who has a physical disability in the study
by Kenny et al. (2000:20): 'There was an attitude if you have something
wrong with you, you don't have to reach the same standards others do.'

In Horgan's (2003:112) study, the school apparently believed that the
young person with a disability would not be able to take examinations:

'It's not that I couldn't do them [exams], they just never gave me a chance to do them and I had seen other people doing exams and I thought, why can't I do them? Every time I asked them, it was like "because" all the time. When I went to Pathfinders [support scheme in Further Education colleges for disabled students], I put the emphasis on them that I want to do an exam in whatever and they said "no problem, go for it", and I left there with GCSEs.'

The young people with disabilities in Horgan's study (2000:117) concluded from their school experiences that:

'No one expects us to do well in exams and go on and have a career or even a decent job. Changing this means challenging a mindset that sees the disability, not the person, and that fails to recognise that while it might take a young person with a disability longer to achieve their goals, we can still do it.'

Stereotypical assumptions and lowered expectations are often linked to negative labelling of individuals and/or class groups. Children and young people with special educational needs are particularly prone to this type of negative labelling. Swain, French and Cameron observed that 'labels are usually bestowed by those who have power and authority ['experts'] upon those who do not'. In addition, there is a real danger that these powerful experts: 'By defining what is considered aberrant the boundaries of what is deemed acceptable (or normal) are marked out' (2003:12). It is quite common for people to be labelled by their impairment – 'she's cerebral palsy', 'he's a paraplegic', 'he's an amputee', even 'she's an epileptic' and 'she's Down Syndrome' – as if the disability designation adequately described the person.

Disability is often characterised as a personal tragedy with disabled children described as 'suffering from' or 'victims of' a particular impairment or enduring medical condition. School responses to an acquired disability (brain tumour), while well-intentioned, can highlight a gulf in understanding the real needs of the person involved:

'I was out for most of fifth year and I actually won student of the year, voted by the students. I always thought it was out of pity and they were only trying to be nice. But when you actually think about it, it was kind of … funny.'

(Kenny *et al.*, 2000:35).

Staff room discourse around individuals and/or groups of children with special educational needs can sometimes be negative and the beginning teacher must distinguish between helpful advice and negative labelling.

FACILITATING ACTIVE PARTICIPATION IN CLASSROOM ACTIVITIES

Facilitating the active participation of children and young people who have special educational needs in classroom activities is a priority for teachers. This will involve structuring classroom activities that support and enhance the participation of these children.

All children, but in particular those who have special educational needs, require explicit support to enable participation. These children often require the teaching of self-help and organisational skills to ensure successful participation. Often when children consistently fail to learn, avoidance strategies will be employed that disrupt the learning of both the individual involved and the whole class. Teachers need to understand and respond appropriately to these avoidance strategies. In addition, the teacher needs to be aware of the access needs of those children and young people who have particular disabilities that may hinder active participation.

ORGANISATIONAL SKILLS

Pupils with special educational needs, as stated earlier, often need to learn how to learn. This involves developing self-help skills that will eventually enable independent learning to occur. Griffin and Shevlin (2007) provide some suggested approaches to support the development and inculcation of organisational skills:

- Provide pupils with a list of learning outcomes that is expected of them after a period of teaching ('at the end of this lesson/period you will be able to…').
- Begin each lesson by outlining the knowledge content or the skill to be learned during that session. This will reassure pupils and they are more likely to participate actively and contribute constructively.
- Provide guidance to learners on how to use their time constructively when tackling a classroom task.

- Teach pupils self-assessment skills so that they can improve their learning efforts to achieve the predicted learning outcomes. (What did I find difficult? What do I need more help with?)

RESPONDING TO AVOIDANCE STRATEGIES

Children and young people who constantly experience failure naturally feel disempowered and eventually lose all sense of motivation. Some will withdraw into themselves and give up trying. Others will adopt 'acting out' misbehaviour to avoid constant failure and to mask the pain of failure and the constant onslaught on their sense of self-worth. As teachers, we need to understand that behaviour is an attempt at communication and pupil anger and aggression derives from inner hurt and pain (McNamara and Moreton, 1995). Naturally, teachers are affected by this display of anger and aggression and may become annoyed and angry themselves but this, while providing a temporary respite, is usually counterproductive and the behaviour can become more extreme.

The work of Alfred Adler (1870–1937) and Rudolf Dreikurs (1897–1972) provides useful insights into the nature of behaviour difficulties. Adler and Dreikurs maintained that young people's primary motivation derives from a drive for autonomy and independence in a world dominated by external adult control. Behaviour difficulties appear to originate in a manifestation by these young people of a sense of inferiority and helplessness. Dreikurs posed the question: What kind of unfulfilled need is being communicated by this young person's behaviour? All children and young people have an unsurpassed urge to 'belong' and through difficult behaviour are attempting to attain this sense of belonging. Dreikurs identified four goals of misbehaviour:

- attention
- power
- revenge
- withdrawal.

Within the confines of this discussion, we will focus on attention-seeking behaviour, probably the most common misbehaviour exhibited in the classroom.

Attention-Seeking Behaviour

Attention-seeking behaviour can range from the child who constantly asks irrelevant questions or makes comments during direct teaching sessions to irritating non-verbal behaviour during quiet work periods, such as tilting back on a chair, making humming noises, distracting other pupils physically or pushing objects off the desk. This kind of behaviour arises from the mistaken belief that reassurance about one's existence and importance in the world can only be obtained by obtaining the teacher's direct attention and *sustaining* that attention on a constant basis. The teacher becomes irritated, reprimands the pupil and focuses directly on the misbehaving pupil. The pupil has achieved her/his primary goal of eliciting and maintaining teacher attention and the teacher response has unwittingly reinforced the pupil belief in the effectiveness of the misbehaviour.

What can be Done to Change the Child's Behaviour?

While it is difficult for the teacher to remain unflustered, there are approaches that can minimise this behaviour while redirecting the natural need of the child to be recognised. It is more effective to identify appropriate and desired behaviour than to draw attention to attention-seeking.

Proximity and reinforcement can be effective in modifying attention-seeking behaviour. The teacher can provide attention and recognition by standing or sitting near the pupil and this type of proximity can also be used to focus or to modify a person's behaviour. The teacher walks slowly towards the misbehaving pupil but does not make eye-contact or give any sign of recognition. Standing near the pupil but facing the rest of the class, the teacher praises the desired behaviour demonstrated by the rest of the class, e.g. 'Thank you all for working on your own and not distracting anyone else. I appreciate that.' Any recognition of the pupil and especially a sarcastic comment (though the teacher may be sorely tempted) will reinforce the misbehaviour.

Quiet proximity can also be used by the teacher when a verbal intervention is required. The teacher approaches the child, speaks quietly to him/her and requests that the desired behaviour is demonstrated, e.g. 'Sean, will you please help me by working on your own for the next five minutes. If you need help just raise your hand.'

There will be occasions when these strategies will not be sufficient and the teacher will need to address these issues with the pupil in a safe situation and at an appropriate and private moment. The teacher can help the pupil to reflect on his/her behaviour and enable them to understand the impact of this behaviour on the classroom learning and interaction and suggest how their attention needs can be facilitated through more appropriate classroom behaviour.

It should be noted that teachers should only engage in the types of action they are comfortable with and this action should be appropriate to the age group involved and aim to defuse rather than exacerbate unwanted behaviour.

INCLUDING CHILDREN WITH DISABILITIES IN CLASSROOM ACTIVITIES

Children and young people who have physical and/or sensory disabilities, for example, require active support to become full participants in classroom activities. Access and attitudinal barriers can make participation conditional or almost impossible. Peer interaction between children with and without disabilities can be dominated by a discourse of need and care as reported by Watson *et al.* (1999:17): 'the non-disabled children behaved not as equals, but as guides or helpers'. Over-reliance by pupils with disabilities on peer support in the absence of appropriate access often skewed peer relationships towards dependence, as one young person observed in the study by Kenny *et. al.* (2000:25):

> 'It was kind of difficult just to get around. And asking for help, I found that difficult. I didn't like asking the same person all the time ... Some people would make a fuss over me and others wouldn't think – it was a mixture of reactions.'

In practical subjects, such as Science and Physical Education, it can be very easy to overlook the need to ensure active participation for pupils with disabilities. In Kenny *et al.* (2003:103), there was evidence of starkly contrasting approaches to involving pupils with physical disabilities in Science lessons. One young person was the passive observer – 'In science, using things on the bench. I just sat down and watched' – yet, in another school, a pupil was actively participating – 'We'd pair up and my partner used to do all the physical work. I just couldn't do it. I couldn't hold a glass of water.'

Again, school practice in relation to physical education varied enormously as the following excerpts illustrate:

- 'I think most of us were excluded especially in sports – the school wasn't equipped to cope. They tried, but the majority of times you had to stay out' (2000:103).
- 'I wasn't excluded from any sports. Actually they pushed me into things more than taking me out – "you are going into this, no questions asked!"' (2000:103).

Exclusion can appear to be natural even to a student with a disability:

'The PE teacher let me watch. There was no discrimination.'
[Q: 'Did they include exercises suited to you?']
'Oh no, no. But he was very good' (2000:104).

By the second phase of the research, the last speaker had revised his viewpoint considerably: 'The nearest I got was inside the hall … He could have let me referee, there's nothing wrong with my mouth' (2000:104).

Extracurricular outings were often planned without considering the needs of young people with physical disabilities and the isolation experienced as a result is evident: 'I would listen to them when they came back – "You missed a great couple of days, we'd great fun." Even sitting beside them hearing them laughing, it was laughing at something you didn't understand. I didn't like that' (Kenny *et. al.* 2000:104).

ENABLING CURRICULUM ACCESS

One of the major aims of special educational provision is providing access to the curriculum for children with special educational needs. Often in response to their learning needs, these children were offered a very limited curriculum that focused on basic skills. While the acquisition of these skills can be useful, the consequent denial of access to large areas of curriculum content was believed to be inequitable and preventing these children from reaching their full potential.

The following example from Byers and Rose (1996:101) illustrates how enabling access to a broader curriculum can enhance learning:

> 'If you'd said to me a few years ago that I'd ever be teaching *Romeo and Juliet* or *Julius Caesar* to my kids, I'd have laughed. I mean, for English we'd mainly been worrying about whether they could fill in an application form or read the destination board on a bus. But now that I'm doing Shakespeare, I wouldn't stop. It's shown what the kids can do if you give them a chance. And there's so much in it for them – not just the language and the heritage stuff, but real, relevant ideas.'

Ensuring curricular access for children and young people with special educational needs represents a considerable challenge for all teachers. Teachers are attempting to balance individual and class needs with the requirement to make progress through the curriculum. Differentiation involves attempting to cater for the individual needs of the pupil while teaching in an ordinary classroom. The teacher has to contend with many factors including large class sizes, a wide range of abilities among learners, and the pressures of preparing pupils for examinations. However, as Griffin and Shevlin (2007:150) maintain, 'the application of the principles and practice of differentiation is fundamental to the skills of successful high-value teaching and learning at any level'.

In Ireland, the NCCA (National Council for Curriculum and Assessment) adopts a comprehensive definition that identifies 'success in learning' as the primary aim of differentiation:

> Differentiation is how a teacher varies content, activities, methodology and resources when taking into account the range of abilities, interests, needs and experiences of students. The purpose of differentiation is to promote students' success in learning. It deals with each student as an individual but is not merely an individualised learning programme that is administered out of context. It values both the teacher and the student.
>
> (NCCA 2002:27)

In the overall context of teaching and learning the Special Education Support Service (SESS) (www.sess.ie) has developed very useful guidelines for teachers attempting to differentiate the curriculum for pupils with special educational needs:

- **Level and pace**: Pupils work at a level and pace appropriate to their ability.
- **Interest**: Learning can be enhanced when pupils choose a topic of interest to themselves, e.g. Topic – bar charts: students select from favourite singer, TV programme, football team.
- **Structure**: Some pupils practise skill independently, others are monitored/supported.
- **Teaching style**: Teacher varies teaching strategies adopted in the classroom, e.g. 'chalk and talk', using ICT or video, research using the internet, class discussion, small group work.
- **Time**: Teacher adapts use of time with class as some pupils work independently, others closely monitored by teacher/SNA.
- **Classroom structure**: Teacher structures groups in class to maximise learning – e.g. some pupils work in pairs, others in groups, others individually – each with a clear purpose and role.

Within the classroom situation the following suggestions for enabling children with special educational needs to access the curriculum have proved helpful in the planning and delivery of lesson content (adapted from Griffin and Shevlin (2007) and Malone and Smith (1996)).

Planning lessons:

- Check textbook and printed material to ensure that it does not exceed pupils' language understanding.
- Anticipate new or difficult vocabulary and explain terms before students meet them in texts and develop a word bank containing key definitions of subject terms.
- Provide clear illustrations and diagrams.
- Remove unnecessary detail from worksheets.

Lesson delivery:

- Allow pupils plenty of time to think before responding to questions – use cues or prompts where responses are required from students. For example, use 'wait time' when requesting an answer and then use a prompt; in written assignments provide initial letter of the answer, or show dashes to show number of letters in a word or words in an answer.
- Repeat information or instructions in a simplified way to help pupil understanding of what is expected.
- Support verbal information or instructions by written materials, drawings and diagrams.
- Highlight important terms or information, e.g. use underlining or capitals.
- Use bullet points and lists instead of paragraphs.
- Use the active rather than the passive voice in written text to assist comprehension, e.g. use 'the man won the race' rather than 'the race was won by the man'.
- Verify understanding by allowing pupils to repeat the information or instructions in their own words.

Assessing pupil learning and pupil progress can be very demanding for the beginning teacher and it can be difficult to find the balance between ensuring that pupils receive recognition for their work and that they are reaching the standard required. Assessment must be an integral part of the planning, delivery and evaluation process employed by the teacher. Usually, this assessment is ongoing and may involve a homework assignment and/or oral questioning and revision of work. More formal assessments of learning generally occur at the conclusion of a major topic.

Teachers need to ask themselves what they hope to achieve from this more formal assessment. What will pupils learn? What will the teacher learn about pupil understanding? What are the implications for revising this topic and for future teaching and learning strategies?

Teachers attempting to differentiate assessment of pupil learning are confronted with some difficult questions:

- How does the teacher guarantee that children with special educational needs are given due recognition for progress in learning though objectively they may not have reached a pass mark for that assessment?
- If the teacher uses a differential marking scheme, how does the teacher ensure that the other children in the class are not disadvantaged in the assessment?
- How can one explain giving 'good' grades to students who are lower achievers on the basis that they have made a 'good effort'?

Teachers can modify the assessment procedures and some of the following approaches could be considered:

- Providing choices in questions, some of which the student with special educational needs can answer successfully.
- Pre-teaching of key assessment tasks.
- Shortening the assignment.
- Allowing more time to complete the task.
- Permitting the assignment task to be presented in a different medium (e.g. audio recording, photo-journal).
- Dictation of the assignment to a scribe (possibly Special Needs Assistant).

Grading assignments can also be modified to take into account the difficulties in learning experienced by children with special educational needs. The following approaches can be considered:

- Employing 'satisfactory/unsatisfactory' as the criteria for grading a piece of work.
- Giving descriptive feedback rather than a grade based on an evaluation of the outcomes achieved by the student (in relation to their individual education plan).
- Providing separate grades for achievement and for effort.

MARKING WRITTEN WORK

Marking written work is an opportunity to provide constructive feedback to the pupil on the strengths and weaknesses of the work. However, as teachers, we need to be very clear about why we are marking the work and whether or not our marking will help or impede pupil progress in learning.

Before any assignment, we need to explain to pupils what is required and model appropriate answers during class. There appears to be confusion about the terms 'marking' and 'correcting' and they are often used interchangeably even though they refer to quite discrete teacher activities.

Marking entails assigning a grade that demonstrates where the work stands in comparison to the pupil's previous work and to her/his peer group. Correcting focuses on improving the text by highlighting mistakes.

Teachers need to be aware that there are many hidden factors that can influence the marking process: spelling is a very influential factor in marking; previous experience of a pupil's work can also be a significant factor; other factors can include handwriting style and legibility, grammar, syntax and sequencing.

As Garnett (1994:8) points out, when assessing an assignment the teacher has to decide 'whether the aim is to check for understanding/knowledge from the written work, as in examinations, tests, finished essays' or 'whether the aim is to achieve understanding/learning through writing as in drafting, note-taking and making, problem solving, thinking in writing'. Examining and grading work is appropriate when the assignment is a test. However, when the aim is to increase understanding, the teacher has a number of options. S/he can act as responsive reader (guiding the pupil), editor (helping the pupil to improve the text), proofreader (correcting mistakes and helping the pupil not to repeat these mistakes).

Children with special educational needs may make many mistakes in their writing and the teacher can find it difficult to determine where to begin in correcting the work. It is probably best to identify a small number of items requiring attention that could be addressed in the next written assignment. Garnett (1994:15) observed the following:

- Few children manage to deal with all their mistakes at once, so correcting them all achieves little.
- Some cannot deal with more than one mistake at a time.
- A written record of this learning enables the child to see how well s/he is doing.
- This gives satisfaction and motivation to achieve more.

Children who have experienced regular failure in learning will need reassurance that this improvement work is not a further failure but rather an indication of more learning required. This approach gives practical support to improve writing skills and enables children with special educational needs to see how the marking is part of a process aimed at enhancing their learning.

While ensuring curricular access through differentiation involves considerable planning and evaluation of progress, the alternative of ignoring the wide variety of abilities in the classroom is not tenable. Differentiated approaches to lesson planning, content delivery and assessment of learning outcomes offer an opportunity to support the real learning needs of children who encounter difficulties in learning and avoid pupil disaffection, disenchantment and entrenched learning failure.

CONCLUSION

Pupils who have special educational needs are all individuals with their own unique strengths and weaknesses and, as teachers, our task is to enable them to become successful learners. This represents a real challenge for all teachers. However, through a combination of knowledge, empathy and collegial support it can be done. Thomas, in the book *Encouraging Voices* (edited by Shevlin and Rose 2003) recounted the value of teacher/adult support as he came to terms with the fact that he has Asperger's Syndrome (at the mild level on the autism spectrum):

> 'At my school I would definitely get help with work such as planning and good content. My teachers want the best for me and they encourage me ... I have a special Learning Support Assistant (LSA) who helps me a lot. She's very patient; I like her. When I had difficulty joining in with others in Year 7, she worked with me and taught me how to do it ... Before I knew I had Asperger's my junior school teachers thought I was a bad boy. The other children teased and bullied me and it was a horrible time. Now I am more confident because more people understand me ... I've had problems with that [being accepted] too, but it's definitely getting better because more people take me as I am. That's because they have learned about me and know what to do for the best, and probably most important I am in a good school.'

SECTION THREE
– DEVELOPING AS A TEACHER

8

Reflective Practice

Rose Dolan

> Consciously, we teach what we know; unconsciously, we teach who we
> are (Hamachek 1999)

INTRODUCTION

Reflection has been described as trying to see the back of your head while
looking in the bathroom mirror (Brookfield 1998), an impossible thing to
do unless you have access to another mirror. In this chapter, we will look at
the roots of reflective practice, the key writers in the area and some
strategies (or mirrors) that will assist in developing the reflective dimension
of your teaching. Before any of that, it is important to consider the rationale
for reflective practice.

WHY REFLECT?

When we observe experienced teachers and look only at what they do, we
miss a fundamental dimension of understanding. Of course, we can
reproduce their actions but this is a bit like watching a great conductor in
front of an orchestra and assuming that waving a stick at a group of
musicians is the totality of the process. Understanding why they do things
in a certain way, what prompted them to adjust the lesson plan halfway
through the class or how they instinctively seem to know what to do in a
situation requires a conversation with the teacher where they explain their
teaching process to us. This is what Donald Schön (1983, 1987, 1992)
described as reflection in action and knowing in action and is used by
Nesbit *et al.* to describe what great teachers do.

> [They] think strategically and act with commitment. When we
> watch these teachers we can see, and admire, their grasp of
> teaching technique. But these teachers have more than skill;

they also think and act at a number of levels. Such teachers have a deep understanding of themselves and their students, and of the organisational contexts in which they work. They think 'on their feet', and take a long term view of their work.

(Nesbit, Leach and Foley 2004:74)

In his seminal book, *The Reflective Practitioner* (1983), Schön indicated that the ability to reflect on action and thus to engage in a process of lifelong learning is one of the defining characteristics of a professional practice. He argued strongly that a model of technical rationality or instrumental problem-solving neither describes nor does justice to the way in which professionals think on their feet and respond to emerging situations and is also ill-suited to the rapidly changing world in which we live and work. Understanding both the problem and its context fundamentally results in a greater possibility of responding more appropriately in our work.

Our preconceived understandings of how teachers and pupils should behave in classrooms are deeply ingrained in us. They come from a variety of sources, for example our own educational histories, media representations of good and bad teaching, and our internalised beliefs about what society requires from teachers, to. name but a few. If these remain unexplored and unchallenged, then our capacity for self-actualisation can be restricted as we occupy an external locus of control (Rotter 1954) and struggle to conform to what is expected of us. Deeply and critically reflecting on ourselves as teachers and on the teaching processes that we use in our classrooms is more likely to lead to better teaching and learning in the classroom and a greater sense of personal satisfaction for you as teacher.

Brookfield gives six reasons for critical reflection in his book *Becoming a Critically Reflective Teacher* (1995). Being critically reflective:

1. **Helps us take informed actions:** If we are asked by pupils, parents or other teachers about why we are doing something, it enables us to offer a thought-out reason for our actions. We tend to have more consistency between our words and our actions. This can also be described as a defensible philosophy of education.

2. **Helps us develop a rationale for practice:** Having a rationale for practice serves as an ethical and pedagogical anchor. It enables us to stay focused as we work in a profession that is highly political and is prone to being buffeted by the changing winds of society. Our rationale, however, is not a fixed entity, it develops and evolves as our experiences grow and as we continue to reflect on them.

3. **Helps us avoid self-laceration:** As teachers, we have a tendency to blame ourselves when things go wrong. As a result, we can (erroneously) believe that we are both the cause and solution to every problem in our classrooms. Being critically reflective enables us to understand the cultural, emotional and political dimensions to resistance in our classrooms and to tackle those issues that are within our own zone of influence.

4. **Grounds us emotionally:** Sometimes we feel very powerful in a classroom, but at other times we are very conscious of our own powerlessness. An unreflective stance can cause us to consider these instances as chance and luck, with fate determining the climate of our classrooms.

5. **Enlivens our classrooms:** As we reflect on our professional practice, it causes us to do things differently. The fact that we are continuing to learn is an important modelling of intellectual enquiry for our pupils. It enables them to see that mistakes are part of the learning process and, if it is built into the classes, it enables them to develop these higher order skills for themselves.

6. **Increases democratic trust:** What we do counts. Our classrooms are places where pupils learn not just about our subjects but also about how to work together, how to achieve, how to be democratic or manipulative. Reflecting on our actions, the assumptions upon which they are built and the way in which they are interpreted by our pupils makes us conscious of the political dimension of the work that we do.

When we have seen our practice through the eyes of others, we no longer teach innocently.

WHAT DO WE MEAN BY REFLECTION?

The concept of reflection is not a new one in educational circles. Nearly eighty years ago, John Dewey wrote *How We Think* and defined reflective thought as 'active, persistent, and careful consideration of any belief or supposed form of knowledge in the light of the grounds that support it and the further conclusions to which it leads'. (Dewey 1933:118). The integral attitudes that he deemed necessary for reflective, critical practice were openmindedness, responsibility and wholeheartedness. This notion of reflective thought was developed further by Donald Schön in 1983. As mentioned earlier, Schön's concept of the reflective practitioner was a significant moment in the description of how professionals think about their work. It began to explain the decision-making processes employed by professionals as they carry out their work. To this end, Schön described two states of reflection:

- Reflection on action.
- Reflection in action.

The process of reflection on action is probably the one that we are most familiar with. When you use this type of reflection, you evaluate a lesson or an action to determine if it achieved its purpose. Based on this evaluation, you adjust your plan for the next class or event. While it involves reflection, there is a danger that it leads to habitualised action if the reflection remains at a relatively superficial level. Sustained critical reflection requires you to go beyond your own frame of reference for understanding and/or solutions.

Reflection in action is the decision-making process that you employ when you make changes on the spot, the kind of thinking on your feet that was described earlier. This tends to be more difficult to describe as it is the result of a number of different factors, most notably your prior experience and ability to accurately read an emerging situation.

Knowledge in action is the term used to describe the implicit knowledge of teaching that informs reflection in action.

Schön's own words capture the distinction between superficial reflection and sustained critical engagement.

> The practitioner allows himself to experience surprise, puzzlement, or confusion in a situation which he finds uncertain or unique. He reflects on the phenomenon before him, and on the prior understandings which have been implicit in his behaviour. He carries out an experiment which serves to generate both a new understanding of the phenomenon and a change in the situation.
>
> (Schön 1983:68)

As the quotation indicates, it is through a process of action and reflection that the practitioner develops and improves practice. While experience is a basis for learning, it must be underpinned by reflection. A spiral of action and reflection is suggested, where the teacher acts, reflects on the action and plans a new action, informed by the reflection. The process, therefore, involves making educated predictions about what will work, based on reflection on prior practice and experience. The concept is spiral rather than cyclical, indicating a deepening of understanding and knowledge as the process is carried out. Sometimes, the spiral does not solve problems but rather raises other perspectives that had not been considered by the teacher in the initial reflection. Schön's own definition of reflective practice involves thoughtfully considering your own experiences in applying knowledge to practice while being coached by professionals in the discipline (Schön 1996). In summary, reflective practice has the following characteristics (see Moore and Ash 2002):

- It is critical.
- It challenges existing assumptions and actively seeks out alternative perspectives.
- It contributes to change or development in a significant way.

Levels of Reflection

When Schön described a process of reflecting on our work as a way of improving practice, he was referring not to single but to double loop learning, a concept he had developed earlier with Argyris (1978). He mentioned the constraint of reflective practice as leading to habitualised action, unless we engage in questioning the context in which the practice is taking place. This dimension of reflection, described as critical reflection (Mezirow 1991), encourages us to reflect on the contradictions and dilemmas that are present in our work. Žižek (2005) describes the concept of parallax views, a dilemma that arises when we are confronted with two incongruent ways of looking at an issue and can only comfortably accommodate one view. It involves the 'confrontation of two closely linked perspectives between which no neutral common ground is possible'. A third dimension of reflective teaching, alluded to in Brookfield's description of the reasons for reflecting, involves the consideration of the political, societal and structural factors that are at play. This is the concept of critical consciousness, generally associated with Paulo Freire (1970).

So reflection can occur in one or all of these dimensions. We can reflect on our practice without questioning the values or assumptions that are behind it. It may challenge the value system that we operate from. It may require us to think about the political, societal and structural factors that underpin the system we find ourselves working in (see the ITT Pilot website, www.ittpilotresources.org.uk).

Argyris and Schön (1978), defining learning as the detection and correction of error, distinguished between what they called single and double loop learning. When we engage in single loop learning, we detect and correct the problem within the existing system and assume that the system is fine. With double loop learning, we look at the assumptions behind what we do and ask if this is the best way of working.

The following example illustrates the contrast between single and double loop learning.

> Last week, I used group work in my classroom and it got quite noisy. The teacher in the next classroom told me later that it disturbed their class.
>
> In single loop learning, the tendency is to fix the problem as it stands. So I might decide not to use group work any more. Equally, I might decide to swap my class into another, more isolated room where there is less likelihood that others will be disturbed.
>
> If I employ double loop learning, I look for immediate solutions but I also begin to question the architecture of schools ('How have so many schools been built that have paper thin walls?') and societal beliefs about learning ('Do we always need silence or quiet to learn?'). I may still fix the problem by swapping classrooms or by discontinuing group work but I do so in a more informed way.

Reflection may also be categorised according to the way in which it is carried out. It can be fleeting, deliberate, or deliberate and systematic (Hall 1997).

- Fleeting reflections tend to be non-evaluative. We may describe what has happened in an anecdotal way or evaluate from a purely personal point of view. This can contribute to deeper levels of reflection by providing the platform for the more deliberate use of reflection.
- Deliberate reflection can be solitary or collaborative. It may take the form of journal writing, critical friend conversations or involvement in small or large group discussions. Although this is reflection on action, as described by Schön, it may not lead to changes in practice, unless it is supported by the third level of reflectiveness.
- Deliberate and systematic reflection tends to be more programmatic and involves action as a support to reflection. Carrying out an action research project or involvement in a subject department review are examples of deliberate and systematic reflection. The use of action research to support reflection is described in more detail later in the chapter.

Table 8.1: Types of Reflection

Types of Reflection	Strengths	Concerns
Reflection in action Thinking on your feet.	Quality and authenticity – you can be yourself.	Absence of another perspective.
Reflection on action Retrospective thinking about your lesson.	Deeper thinking because there is time. Capacity to stimulate improvement in future practice.	More effective when supported by writing. Can become a negative cycle of brooding.
Written evaluations Usually written after individual lessons and focusing on pupil and teacher performance.	Helpful to have a framework for reflection.	Criteria are constructed by someone else. Can be a pen-pushing exercise.
Professional verbalised reflections Can be conversations with those in the professional field (teachers, fellow students, supervisors, lecturers, pupils) or those within support networks (friends and family).	Open up different perspectives on incidents or show other ways of thinking.	Important to find the right people to reflect with. Finding time for conversations. Potential for competition with other students.

(Adapted from Moore and Ash 2002)

Strategies for Promoting Reflection

Your initial teacher education programme provides many opportunities for reflection; some opportunities are formally designed and others occur unintentionally. Your own interest in specific issues may be raised by lectures in the foundation disciplines: educational psychology, the history of education, the philosophy of education, or the sociology of education. Areas that relate to curriculum studies or pedagogical skills and theory may also raise questions that prompt reflection. Formal assignments generally have a reflective dimension built into them. Discussions with your teaching practice supervisors can also be a prompt for reflecting on your teaching and the context in which it occurs.

Below are a number of different strategies that you can use to gather information about your teaching and the value or belief system that underpins it.

Deliberate Strategies
* Keeping a reflective journal.
* Analysis of your own autobiography as a learner and teacher.
* Audio taping or videotaping your classes (this requires permission from school and pupils).
* Being observed by and/or observing a colleague.
* Attendance at workshops and seminars.
* Teaching portfolios.

Moving from deliberate to deliberate and systematic strategies generally requires a conversation with or input from another person in order to provide a different perspective. This prevents the reflection from becoming bogged down in self-pity or self-laceration.

Deliberate and Systematic Strategies
* Asking your pupils for feedback.
* Action research.
* Formal supervision of your teaching.
* Critical incident analysis.
* Engaging a critical friend.
* Whole school evaluation and subject inspections.

(Brookfield 1997; Hall 1997)

KEEPING A REFLECTIVE JOURNAL

In this section, you'll find more details about using the reflective journal and critical incidents, things to consider when assembling a teaching portfolio and how to employ action research in your classroom.

When you think about keeping a reflective journal, there are a number of questions that probably come to mind.

1. What's the purpose of keeping a journal?
2. Who's going to read it?
3. What do I write in the journal?
4. When do I write the journal?

Keeping a reflective journal may be part of your course requirements, and you may be asked to submit it at the end of the year. This will vary depending on the nature and purpose of the journal on your particular course. However, the main purpose of the journal is to provide you with the opportunity to keep track of your thinking and reflection about your professional practice. You might use it to:

- Record things that have happened as you teach (critical incidents).
- Record strategies or ideas about things you want to do in class.
- Keep track of your ideas as they develop and change over the duration of your course.

Critical incidents are events in your professional life as a teacher that cause you to stop and think about what you are doing. They may be positive or negative. When you write in your journal about a critical incident, it is helpful to do so in three stages.

1. Describe what happened. Include what you did and what the pupils did.
2. Analyse the event by considering:
   - What went well and why.
   - What went poorly and why.
3. Link your learning to an action plan. How will you use what you have learned in the future?

Some student-teachers find that the act of keeping a journal about a negative critical incident enables them to gain perspective on the incident and, through discussing the analysis with a critical friend or trusted colleague, enables them to move on from it in a non-destructive way.

In order to use your journal as a reflective tool, it is important to reread your entries at regular intervals and to actively look for common themes in your writing. Use a highlighter to identify themes such as:

- My beliefs about teaching and learning.
- Working with colleagues.
- Communication with parents.
- My professional skills.
- My subject knowledge.

You should now consider how you can deepen the reflective process through strategies like the ones mentioned earlier, e.g. critical friend conversation or discussion with a supervisor or tutor.

THE TEACHING PORTFOLIO

Portfolios have a long tradition among many professionals such as artists, photographers, journalists, architects and writers but their use in teaching is a recent phenomenon. A portfolio is a place where you can gather together the evidence of your teaching accomplishments. These might include samples of pupils' work, pieces of reflective writing, video or audio recordings of classes or a series of lesson plans. Although a portfolio could be considered as a receptacle for evidence of teaching, it can also be used as a tool for reflection (Lyons *et al.* 2002). The reflective component of the teaching portfolio occurs as you make decisions about what to include, what to omit and why. As you choose the contents of your portfolio, ask yourself:

- What am I putting in?
- What am I leaving out?
- Why?
- What does this tell me and others about my teaching?

It is in writing the rationale for inclusion and exclusion that you engage in the reflective process as you begin to examine what you have learned from the experience represented by the artefact.

ACTION RESEARCH

'Action research' is a term used to describe the way in which professionals research their own practice in order to understand and improve it. As you learn to teach, it is worth engaging in this type of research in order to both understand your practice and to effect change.

It encourages you to make use of yourself, your colleagues and your pupils as well as the theoretical literature to develop your practice as a teacher. It integrates with reflective practice through a process of identification and response. While reflective practice can be used to identify problems, action research can seek to provide solutions (McMahon 1999). Some of the underlying tenets of action research involve the recognition of your importance in the process. This is not the type of research that requires you to observe and report: you are at the centre of the process, asking a real question about a real issue to which you want to find a solution. As you engage in the research, you are trying to bring about some improvement in your practice, no matter how small (McNiff *et al.* 1996). Although there are many definitions of action research, what they all have in common is that it involves enquiring into your own practice through a cyclical process which involves planning, acting, observing and reflecting (Kemmis and McTaggart 1988).

How do you undertake action research? A simple action research project would look something like this:

1. **Identify the area of concern or the performance gap:** This is the discrepancy between what you want to do and what you are actually doing (Hopkins 1993).

   You can identify this in a number of different ways, including: critical incidents that happen in your classroom; feedback from supervisors, colleagues or pupils; entries in your reflective journal; and video and audio recordings of your classroom. These strategies enable you to collect information or evidence about what is going on in your classroom. Identify something that is of concern to you, something that you can or wish to do something about.

   When you have identified the area of concern, begin to consider the causes of the performance gap. This enables you to identify possible solutions. The source of these solutions should be from fellow student-teachers, supervisors, co-operating teachers and from reading. This engages you in a process that integrates reflection with planning for action and moves you beyond the single loop learning referred to earlier. Collaborative critical conversations are very important components of the process. Indeed, if you can find a colleague with the same area of concern, it enables a more collaborative approach to be taken.

2. **Devise a plan for improvement:** When you have considered possible solutions, choose the most appropriate ones, i.e. those that are fit-for-purpose. Since you are the expert on this class and this topic at this time, it is important that you devise a plan that you can implement, one that will address your area of concern.

3. **Implement the plan:** As you put your plan into action, keep a note of the effects of the plan on teaching and learning in your classroom and of the changes that you observe in your classroom.

4. **Collect evidence that demonstrates improvement:** It could be an improvement in the pupils' written work or in the classroom environment. This moves you beyond the individual reflective approach, requiring you to seek out concrete evidence that supports your claim of improvement. If you are feeling particularly brave, look for what Magee (1982) calls the 'disconfirming instances', actively seeking evidence that does not support your claim of improvement. Popper maintained that while we can easily find evidence that proves our theories, attempting to disprove our theories and failing to do so is a stronger validation of the theory.

   Reappraise your practice in light of the goals that you have set for the action research project. Have these goals been achieved? Totally?

Partially? Not at all? Have there been unanticipated outcomes to the action research?

5. **Share the results of your action research with other student teachers, with your supervisors and/or with your co-operating teachers:** Invite them to comment on your results, to offer alternative interpretations and to make suggestions for further action. This is possibly the most difficult part of action research as the culture of schools has not traditionally lent itself to these kinds of conversation.

6. **Amend the plan and repeat the steps:** Note that this time the concern or performance gap may be different from the original one. As you engage in the process of action research, you uncover different areas of your practice that you wish to improve.

Action research is also effective as an evaluative process, but its real strength lies in its potential to reduce the sense of isolation that teachers experience, to empower teachers to initiate change and to promote professional development. Above all, it recognises your fundamental role as a teacher in making decisions about classroom practice that are based upon the needs of your students (Atherton 2005).

CHALLENGES TO REFLECTION

Reflective practice, although not a new concept, is now a significant component of initial teacher education programmes, not only in Ireland but also in the international educational community. You are encouraged to become a reflective practitioner by the education departments of universities and colleges, by the Department of Education and Science and by the Teaching Council.

However, being a reflective practitioner brings challenges with it, not insurmountable challenges but challenges nonetheless. These include a lack of time, stress and anxiety, the volume of new experiences to reflect upon and reflection that is subject to formal assessment or evaluation (Moore and Ash 2002). Societal expectations of what teachers do and isolation can also militate against being reflective, as can attachment to routine, particularly when reflection becomes 'routinised' and ritualistic. As we become accustomed to the routine of the school, the classroom and the expectations on us as teachers, we cease to see things that are out of place. It's like moving into a new house or apartment. We put things in temporary places with the intention of putting them away later. Initially, these out of place items may preoccupy us but as time passes, we not only cease to see them but we assume a normality about their placing. It's only when we look with the eyes of others that we see that these things are misplaced and that something needs to change.

In our classrooms, these temporary things may be a preoccupation with coping strategies rather than considered approaches, with classroom management to the exclusion of curriculum and pedagogy, with methods of teaching that are focused solely on learning for exams and, most critically of all, with a loss of the very things that attracted us to teaching in the first instance.

Adopting a critically reflective stance to teaching did not begin or end with Dewey or Schön. Its roots are present in Socratic thinking and in Platonic writing (Hogan *et. al.* 2007) and it continues to occupy the education agenda in the twenty-first century. It challenges us as professionals to deepen our understanding of what we do. It involves a commitment to remaining open to learning throughout our teaching careers.

> This involves not just keeping up with changes in the syllabus or with relevant developments in the subjects one is teaching. It also involves learning from one's colleagues and from one's students, among others, about the effects of one's own teaching, about short-comings as well as strengths in one's own practice, about the helpful as distinct from the hindering contributions students can make, about an abundance of ideas unthought of before in one's own mind.
>
> (Hogan *et al.* 2007:41)

It requires us to learn to teach, not in a technical-rational manner by simply learning some recipes for action or relying solely on a bag of tricks, but by responding to the context in which we work so that we teach in a way that is not innocent but that embodies the qualities described by Dewey: openmindedness, responsibility and wholeheartedness.

KEY QUESTIONS AND EXERCISES FOR REFLECTIVE PRACTICE

Reflective Journal Writing

A useful starting point is to think about your own educational history or your learning autobiography. Choose one of the questions below and write the answer to it in your reflective journal. Choose a different question each week. After a few weeks, reread your answers and look for themes. Use a highlighter to draw attention to recurring themes or patterns. If you prefer to keep an electronic journal, use the on-screen highlighter or choose different font colours to highlight the recurring themes.

1. What has been the most memorable class/lecture you attended as a student? It might be primary, post-primary or college. Describe it in as much detail as possible. What are the characteristics of that learning experience?
2. Think about something that you learned outside of school. How did you learn? Did you learn on your own or did someone teach you? Describe it in as much detail as possible. What are the characteristics of that learning experience?
3. When have you found learning really difficult? What made it difficult?
4. Think about the teacher(s) who influenced you most in the course of your education. Was it a positive or negative influence? List their qualities. What attitudes and skills did your most memorable teacher possess?
5. How similar/different is the school you are teaching in to the school you attended? (If you are teaching in the school that you attended as a pupil, what have you learned about the school since you made the transition from pupil to teacher?) How does the class that you were in compare to the classes that you are now teaching?
6. What do good teachers do? What do good pupils do? How does learning happen? What are the values that you consider important in education? What is important to you in teaching and learning?
7. What effect has your educational history had on how you teach?

Critical Incidents

When a critical incident happens, write about it using the following headings.

1. Describe what happened. Include what you did and what the other people involved in the incident did.
2. Analyse the event by considering:
   – What went well and why.
   – What went poorly and why.
3. Link your learning to an action plan. How will you use what you have learned in the future?

To deepen the reflection, ask yourself the following questions (adapted from www.ittpilotresources.org.uk):

1. Is this about changing my practice?
2. Does this situation challenge my value-system? (If so, you may want to think about how you feel in relation to it and why.)
3. Is it a situation outside my immediate sphere of influence and control? (In this situation, you may wish to question the political or economic forces and values lying behind it.)

Writing a Case Study

In order to employ this reflective technique, you need to work with another student-teacher. Write a description of a classroom situation. This situation may have happened to you or you may have observed the situation. Include as much detail as possible. You might want to include the following information:

- A description of the teacher in terms of age and experience.
- A description of the school.
- A description of the students.
- When and where the situation occurred.
- Who was involved.

Your description should not include the solution or outcome of the situation that you have described. Exchange your case study with another student teacher. Write your response to their situation. Your response should include:

- Your analysis of the situation. What are the underlying causes?
- Your recommended solution.
- An explanation of why you are recommending this course of action.

Return the case study and your response to the other student-teacher. Retrieve their response to your situation. Read it with an open mind, paying special attention to their analysis and explanation. Have a conversation with them about their response. Write your reflection about the conversation in your journal, with particular reference to the different perspective that they brought to the situation.

HELPFUL WEBLINKS FOR REFLECTIVE PRACTICE

- Reflective Teaching Web is an excellent site containing free resources for reflective classroom practice. It is linked to Andrew Pollard's books on reflective teaching (www.rtweb.info).
- This site contains information sheets, activities and video footage for student teachers (excellence.qia.org.uk/GoldDust/reflectivepractice/reflective.html).

- James Atherton's Reflective Practice website gives further information about Schön and Argyris. It also contains links to other theorists, such as Kolb/Lewin and the learning cycle (www.learningandteaching.info/learning/reflecti.htm).
- This site's main page offers a menu that links to classroom teaching and learning (www.learningandteaching.info).

9

Teaching Practice and Beginning Teaching

Brendan Walsh

INTRODUCTION

This chapter is divided into two parts:

- **Teaching practice supervision: some guidelines for the student-teacher:** This section deals with the issue of teaching practice supervision. The procedure and evaluation of supervision differs between initial teacher education institutions and we offer only general guidelines for approaching this process.
- **Beginning teaching: your first year:** This section deals with the common challenges facing newly qualified teachers (NQTs) as they begin their teaching career. It is based on research specific to Ireland, looks at those issues that are of interest to school principals, the common difficulties faced by NQTs and offers advice on how to approach them.

TEACHING PRACTICE SUPERVISION: SOME GUIDELINES FOR THE STUDENT TEACHER

Teaching practice is usually guided and supervised by an internal and/or external supervisor attached to the teacher education institute. It is a critical and invaluable experience for the student-teacher and should be approached in a spirit of co-operation and willingness to learn. While student-teachers will already have a sense of the methodologies and approaches they wish to employ, it is important that they remain open to the variety and richness of the critical voices they will encounter during the degree/diploma period.

Occasionally, student-teachers report feeling confused as they are presented with what appears to be an array of contradictory methodologies.

As already outlined, there is no single way to teach and different methodologies and approaches will suit different teachers, pupils, types of school, subjects, classroom environments and group dynamics.

Supervision as Support

While it is tempting to concentrate on the evaluative aspect of the supervision process, you should also try to view it as a type of mentoring, a guided introduction into the community of teaching. Supervision represents a learning opportunity for both parties and, while it is evaluative, the student-teacher should seek a co-operative relationship, keeping in mind that the supervisor is a professional educator with substantial teaching experience.

The supervisory visit is a means of support and the student-teacher should approach it in this spirit, seeking to:

* become proactive
* make suggestions
* critically comment on success and failure
* demonstrate a critical capacity to evaluate progress between visits
* suggest new ways of progressing.

Supervisors will look to see if students are developing the ability to reflect critically upon their teaching – seeking ways of improving the learning opportunities of their pupils and themselves. Hence, supervision is concerned, at one level, with the development and critical employment of methodology and with the development of a detached objective and constructive approach to the development of the craft of teaching. It is a collaborative venture – a process of planning and evaluation. A reflective, proactive student will eagerly anticipate the supervisory visit as an opportunity to plan, test ideas, query, share successes and seek advice.

What are the Outcomes of Teaching Practice Placement?

Teaching practise placement should result in the following outcomes:

* The practice of skills required for particular discipline.
* The development of best practice.
* The integration of teacher education content with pupil learning.
* The articulation of a vision statement for yourself and your discipline.
* Appreciation of the need for Continuing Professional Development (CPD).

Supervision and teaching practice placement should work towards the fulfilment of these goals and it is worth revisiting them during the degree/diploma year in order to remind yourself of the purpose of your journey. Of course, supervisors will seek to establish whether or not learning has taken place during an observed lesson. If the student-teacher has based his/her methodology, aims and objectives around this single central outcome, then evidence of learning should be obvious. Student-teachers should not be surprised to be asked what, if any, pupil learning took place during the lesson and how can they know with certainty that this was so.

Procedures for Teaching Practice Supervision: General Guidelines

Usually, your supervisor will arrive at your school approximately ten to fifteen minutes before your lesson. While practices differ between institutions – and you should familiarise yourself with how your department operates – the supervisor will usually arrive without prior notice. You may be asked to produce your lesson plans dating to the beginning of the year/term/week or just for that day. The supervisor may also ask for an explanation of the plan and clarification of issues arising from it. If possible, this meeting should take place in a separate room and not in the staff room. This will enable you or the supervisor to raise any challenging issues or concerns – a precaution taken out of respect for and in order to protect your privacy and that of your pupils.

The Supervisor in the Classroom: General Conduct and Procedure

When your supervisor is happy to proceed, you should take him/her to your classroom and ensure that an appropriate seat is made available. The supervisor may elect to sit in a particular location. As a rule, this should be where s/he cannot be overlooked by pupils, enabling written observations to remain private. As a matter of courtesy, the supervisor should be introduced to your pupils, when they have settled. There is no need to explain why s/he is present other than that he/she is 'sitting in' on the lesson. When you have started your lesson there is no need to involve the supervisor in any other way and, depending upon the procedure in your teacher education college/university, the supervisor, generally, will not interrupt or comment on your lesson.

Should I Follow my Lesson Plan Rigidly?

The lesson plan, as discussed in Chapter 2, is not written in stone and, even under supervision, you should not feel restricted by it should genuine opportunities for learning and exploration arise during a lesson. Your supervisor will be keen to see whether or not you identify such opportunities and to what extent you maximise their potential. You need to develop the ability to think on your feet, to be guided, rather than dictated to, by the lesson plan. Should your supervisor enquire about your deviation from the plan, it is not usually meant as a criticism, rather s/he is hoping that you can provide a pedagogically reason for doing so. Very few things delight teaching practice supervisors as much as innovation.

Speaking with your Supervisor after the Observed Lesson

Generally, your supervisor will remain in the room until the end of the lesson and the pupils have dispersed or you are ready to leave. You should not be tempted, under any circumstances, to try to inveigle your supervisor into speaking about possible teaching practice grades for the lesson. While some institutions may differ, as a rule this is frowned upon. Again, institutions have different procedures for the 'debriefing' session following observation, but you might consider the following.

- The post-observation feedback session should take place in private.
- It should be a collaborative session.
- The supervisor's evaluative role is based on his/her expertise in teaching and initial teacher education and the student-teacher should be anxious to receive advice and seek clarity where this is unclear.
- It is unwise to enter into disputes regarding methodology and general practice with your supervisor, although this is not unknown (see below). Occasionally, enthusiasm can cloud judgement and we have yet to encounter a situation when the supervisor's advice was not pedagogically sound, both for the student-teacher and his/her pupils. It is important, therefore, to listen carefully to your supervisor, to makes notes of his/her suggestions and to agree or identify those aspects s/he wishes to see improved upon at the next visit. You should, of course, ask for advice on how these aims might be achieved, but the discussion should end with clear agreement on what you must attend to before the next observation.

How do I Proceed after the Supervisory Visit?

When you have time, you should find a quiet place and revise the notes you made during the conversation with your supervisor. In order of priority, list the recommendations s/he made and begin to reflect on how you might go about developing these in practice. They may be uncomplicated, such as requiring children to raise their hands before asking or answering a question, or more advanced, such as the development of higher-order questioning for a senior group.

When you have identified the topics requiring attention, you must decide, possibly relying upon advice from your supervisor, on how to go about making these changes. These can be so diverse that we will not attempt to offer advice here other than to emphasise the importance of ensuring that you realise what it is you need to concentrate on and devising strategies for achieving them. You may wish to discuss these, as general principles, with your co-operating (mentor) teacher, staff within the college/university or your peers, perhaps at tutorials or workshops. Again, if s/he is agreeable, you may wish to contact your supervisor to 'run' your plans by him/her.

It is very likely that, at the next supervisory visit, the supervisor will be particularly attentive to those areas commonly agreed upon as needing attention at the last visit. If you like, you can remind the supervisor of them and of the action you have taken to make progress in the meantime. This is an excellent opportunity to speak about any challenges (and successes) that presented themselves during this process and how you overcame them, which demonstrates your commitment and engagement. Of course, if there is little or no evidence of this improvement during the observed lesson, you may have to explain the lack of any tangible evidence to support your claims!

What do I do if I Disagree with the Supervisor's Assessment of a Lesson?

If you feel your supervisor has given you unreliable advice or has been unfairly critical of your teaching, preparation or any other aspect of teaching practice, you should, if it is not possible to speak with the supervisor, make an appointment to meet with the director of teaching practice or the chair of the diploma/degree at your college/university.

While this is not common, students can feel aggrieved and seek clarity or reassurance after an unhappy visit/observation. However, students should be aware that it is common practice in almost all colleges/universities to entertain reservations only on the grounds of procedure and not content. In other words, complaining that the supervisor pointed out too many weakness in your teaching is unlikely to get a sympathetic hearing from your institution, whereas pointing out that your supervisor left the lesson before it was complete (and therefore did not observe an entire lesson) would be a sound basis for a complaint upon grounds of procedure – providing attendance for the duration of the lesson was applicable.

BEGINNING TEACHING: YOUR FIRST YEAR

Continuing as a Learner

Newly qualified teachers should be under no illusion as to just how much there is to learn about teaching and learning. The time allotted to initial teacher education diplomas in Ireland is wholly inadequate, but, in the face of political indifference, academics and students must make the most of the one-year allocation. It is important that students realise that only so much can be learned in such a short space of time.

While this is true of all university courses, it is particularly important in the area of professional preparation programmes. Exposure to actual classroom teaching is part of every initial teacher education course: however, this can often be for only two or so hours per week, does not usually enable exposure to examination groups and, depending upon its operation, may mean that students do not see their pupils for two or three days at a time. Hence, such courses can only give a glimpse of teaching life, the reality can be quite different and NQTs can quickly become worn out by workload, pressure and expectation.

You are not Alone

Before dealing in detail with ways in which you might approach your first year of teaching, it is worth remembering that you are not alone. There may be other recently qualified teachers working in your school, you may have friends in other schools and, of course, there are hundreds of 'first timers' throughout the country dipping their feet in the uncertain waters of classroom teaching. Therefore, your anxieties, along with your optimism and willingness, are common characteristics of NQTs everywhere. What you must learn to do is plan for the year ahead, discover what is achievable and what might be left for another time, decide on basic rules and expectations, plan for teaching specific content knowledge and be assured that no one expects more than honest commitment to work hard and the ability to take advice.

Remember, when entering a new school, you are not simply taking up a job, you are entering a community, and many of its members have been there for several years and have gained invaluable insight and wisdom. They have accumulated what might be called 'folk' knowledge of teaching, they relate to their pupils and teach in ways that appear effortless, calm and friendly, and you wish you knew the secret to this relationship. It will come, but, as with all relationships and expertise, you have to earn it.

Before looking in detail at the specific challenges facing newly qualified teachers, it is worth considering a few simple points.

- **If you don't know – ask:**
  As a new member of staff, the so-called learning curve is quite steep. Schools are very busy places and research would indicate that new members of staff only have a short period of 'grace' before they are expected to have a good command of the school and its workings. It is important that you gain a good knowledge of the school layout, regulations, procedures, timetables and general workings as soon as possible. However, if you are uncertain, ask. There is nothing to be gained from operating in ignorance and you may make errors or cause confusion.

  If you are given responsibility, such as a class assembly or roll-call, ensure that you understand exactly what is expected of you, what paperwork is needed and to whom it should go afterwards. In the beginning, do not be tempted to rely on the goodwill of older pupils to guide you through these small duties. Even if you are uncertain, you need to give the impression of confident familiarity in front of your pupils. Of course, you can ask them where a resource is normally kept, or how to operate a piece of equipment, but, for now, you should know how administrative tasks operate.

- **Dress – formal or informal?**
  New teachers should dress appropriately. As a general rule, dress according to the standard of the school. If this is informal, you should follow suit and vice versa. However, principals generally prefer it if staff are not too informal. At any rate, your clothes should be presentable. Standards of dress have changed considerably in schools over the past two decades, but new teachers should avoid obvious informality and as a rule of thumb is it better to dress 'up' than 'down'. New teachers should also keep in mind the ethos and values of the school. This remains important, and there may be expectations around dress codes in particular institutions that you should be sympathetic to.

- **Be prepared:**
  If possible, before the start of the year, ensure that you have furnished yourself with the basic resources you will need. These will differ depending on your subject area, but items such as a Teacher's Journal, pens, rulers, markers and so on should be purchased before the first day. Over the summer, you will have familiarised yourself with the course textbooks and this will have given you an opportunity to design new resource material or fall back upon materials designed or employed during your teaching practice placement.

- **Getting the balance:**
  It is important that you mix optimism with caution. The enthusiasm and

eagerness you feel is natural and laudable, but the first few years of teaching are challenging and it is important that newly qualified teachers have a sense of what can and cannot be achieved. The crucial aspect of this year is gaining thorough knowledge of your content area and devising ways to help pupils to master it; in other words teaching and learning. This is the solid foundation upon which to build your teaching career. Your pupils' primary expectation is that you will help them learn; in the same way that a patient's expectation is that their doctor will help them recover. Bedside manner is secondary! Your school principal will have the same expectation and s/he will know whether or not this is the case.

- **Extracurricular activities: how much?**
The newly qualified teacher should carefully consider the extent to which s/he will become involved in extracurricular activities. There is always tension between a person's willingness to become involved and the need to make time for preparation and marking. If possible, choose an activity where you can make a worthwhile contribution or in which you have some expertise. With time, you will find that schoolwork takes less time and you will be better able to achieve a balance between it, extracurricular activities and your own personal life.

Dealing with Homework

Having thought about how to allocate time in terms of the yearly plan, you need to consider the time you will spend each day/evening on schoolwork. There is no fixed rule for this as workloads, disciplines and the nature of homework differ considerably. For example, teaching a Leaving Certificate English or History group tends to generate very significant amounts of written work for correction.

While it is essential that homework is corrected and returned promptly, the beginning teacher should realise that, if s/he were to correct the homework of eight groups (periods) each day with an average of twenty-five pupils in each group, this would result in approximately two hundred assignments. Obviously, this is impractical and the beginning teacher might remember this figure when s/he hears complaints about insufficient homework being allocated and corrected by teachers! Homework, as previously noted, must support what has been covered in lessons and prepare for and lead to new learning.

Homework differs considerably from one age group to another. A Leaving Certificate group assignment in essay form is a wholly different task from simple multiple-choice questions for a first-year group. There are several approaches to overseeing the quality of assignments. Importantly, all homework should be seen on a regular basis. Many teachers will 'do' homework on the blackboard, enabling pupils to follow and make corrections, if necessary, in their jotters.

This approach is usually quite informal and pupils are encouraged to ask questions, offer alternative solutions and suggestions and discover where and how errors were made. However, the teacher cannot be certain that all are learning from this method unless the pupils' work is collected and scrutinised. This need not be done nightly, but should be done regularly. Again, the teacher can look over this work while the pupils are engaged in individual class work, which may be done by moving from pupil to pupil, or when sitting at your desk. This has the advantage of enabling you to discuss aspects of the work that individuals are finding difficult.

Another method of addressing homework, and also feedback from examinations, is to prepare an overall 'strengths and weaknesses' presentation. This works well for more complex senior level disciplines, where older pupils are able to engage in a more open discussion around texts, solutions or issues.

When individual assignments have been corrected, annotated and returned, the teacher should compile a summary of common errors and misunderstandings along with those issues/aspects that have been intelligently managed. In reading pupils' work and preparing feedback, the teacher should be able to identify repeated misunderstandings. This usually indicates that s/he has presented some issue/aspect erroneously, vaguely or insufficiently. If this happens, it is useful to ask the pupils about how they arrived at this understanding. This usually highlights where the teaching error has occurred and you can then correct it for the group. As a rule of thumb, if a sizeable minority, say 10–15 per cent, of pupils produce the same incorrect answer or misunderstanding, the teacher should suspect an error in teaching and set about rectifying it.

The importance of returning annotated homework promptly cannot be overemphasised. Most pupils are contentious about homework and they deserve to have it corrected fully and returned promptly. Underlying this, of course, is the fact that homework relates to what is being covered in class, so the longer you fail to return it, the more irrelevant it becomes. At the very least, teachers are obliged to ensure that pupils complete homework assignments. A record of this should be kept and followed up. Schools and teachers will have different ways of dealing with pupils who fail to submit homework, but a good rule of thumb is that homework should be completed within a reasonable time. It is important to choose your battles and when a pupil has genuinely forgotten to submit homework, why not simply allow him/her to present it the following day? What is important is that the work is done and done to the best of the pupil's ability.

Principals' Expectations

In 2006, the Department of Education and Science published the first comprehensive survey of the needs of newly qualified teachers. The report presented the findings of the National Pilot Project on Teacher Induction and represents the research findings of teacher educators at St Patrick's College (primary teachers) and University College Dublin (post-primary teachers).

There is no formal, systemic induction system for newly qualified teachers in Ireland and the report emphasises both the effects of this omission and the need to introduce induction to both primary and post-primary strands. In response to a question regarding which areas school principals would like to see included in any future induction support programme for post-primary teachers they responded as follows.

Table 9.1

Content Area	Rank
Discipline and classroom management	1
Dealing with students	2
Awareness of school procedures/policy	3
Awareness of school ethos/culture	4
Teaching methodology	5
Staff relationships	6
Professionalism	7
Lesson preparation	8
Conflict resolution	9
Special needs and mixed ability teaching	10
Professional aspects of teaching position	11
Communication skills and motivating students	12
Assessment	13
Stress management	14
Extracurricular activities	15
Reflective practice	16
Learning by observation of experienced teachers	17
Impact of multiculturalism	18

(Source: NPPTI Report, DES 2006, Table 4.10)

It is noteworthy that discipline and classroom management were prioritised and that teaching methodology, i.e. the methods employed in helping pupils to learn, is almost a third down the list, indeed, below knowledge of school ethos and culture. It is also interesting, given the emphasis on terminal examination in Ireland, that 'assessment' is ranked thirteenth out of eighteen items and reflects that those professionally involved in education appreciate its wider implications and priorities.

CONCERNS OF NEWLY QUALIFIED TEACHERS

When 312 newly qualified teachers were asked to rank the areas of support they would like to see included in any future national programme they responded as follows.

Table 9.2

Area	Rank
Pupils with special needs	1
Pupil behaviour and discipline	2
Motivating and interesting pupils	3
Classroom management and organisation	4
Parent-teacher meetings	5
Preparation of tests and assessment	6
Staff relationships	7
Preparation of content and materials	8

(Source: NPPTI Report, DES 2006, Table 4.20)

The mainstreaming of children with special educational needs has added a new dimension to Irish classrooms. Newly qualified teachers should be aware that issues surrounding discipline and classroom management are always considered crucial in the early months of teaching and that, while problems occur throughout a teacher's career, these tend to become much more manageable as time passes.

Working with Parents

Another area singled out by newly qualified teachers was that of preparing for parent–teacher meetings. It would be more proper to speak of parent–teacher relations, as, usually, we will develop positive working relationships with parents during the time their child or children are in school. Remember, the notion of the parent as primary educator is a deep-seated understanding within Irish education. It is useful to keep this in mind, as it implies that not only do teachers have a grave responsibility, but parents also have a serious duty. It is, therefore, a partnership of separate but complementary roles, the common aim being the welfare and development of the child.

Parent–Teacher Meetings

The parent–teacher meeting is a valuable chance to exchange information and provide expert advice. These meetings now take place in the late afternoon or evening and are onerous for all concerned. Parents often stand in queues for hours to see the relevant teachers, who may be required to meet sixty or more people.

Usually, parents simply wish to know how their child is 'getting on'. However, given what we have already said about partnership, it is important that the teacher establishes to what extent parents are facilitating the child's progress. For example, do they check over homework/the school journal in the evening? Does the child have an appropriate place for study? Do they discuss school progress at home? Do they encourage the child by looking through assignments and tests? It is important that parents realise that they, too, have a key role to play in their child's progress and that they can facilitate it in simple ways. By asking questions such as these, the teacher is able to get an insight into how supportive, or otherwise, parents actually are.

When preparing to meet parents, remember that they, too, may carry assumptions about you, your subject, teachers, schooling and, perhaps, unhappy memories of their own time in school. Before the meeting begins, the teacher should be thoroughly prepared in terms of having collected relevant grades from assignments and tests, should have reflected upon the pupil's classroom contribution and behaviour, general disposition and engagement, and ways in which the pupils can improve any or all of the above. This last aspect is important: a reflective teacher will have given it some thought and parents have a legitimate expectation that s/he will be able to advise them on how to help their child proceed. Parents should not be simply presented with a list of difficulties, as they have probably had to sit through the same list a number of times already. While admitting to the challenges posed by their child, the teacher should also discuss the potential for change and offer solid, sensible advice on how that might be achieved.

These meetings are a time to present a balanced picture and, if there is 'bad' news to be given, then it should be 'sandwiched' between positive feedback, in other words, the teacher should start and end with an upbeat tone. Remember, always, that the person being discussed is not simply another pupil, but an individual child, and that parents see a side of his/her personality that teachers may never glimpse, including his/her insecurity, lack of self-belief, emotional dependence, fear or loneliness. Hence, parents often identify a problem long before the teacher and simply want some advice on how they might go about helping their child. This may appear onerous to the newly qualified teacher and s/he should leave parents in no doubt that the only professional advice s/he can confidently offer relates to learning: we are not experts in the fields of adolescent psychology.

Do not wait until the parent–teacher meeting to bury parents under an avalanche of complaints about their child, particularly if these include serious incidents. Parents, quite rightly, will want to know why you have waited this long to inform them of wayward behaviour or disengagement. As noted in Chapter 3, you should employ the various avenues open to you in contacting parents when necessary.

Finally, it is important that parents understand that you expect them to facilitate and support you in your work, that they trust you to make professional and informed decisions to do with teaching and learning and that you expect them to respect your expertise.

You are not 'answerable' to parents for your methods and pedagogical approaches; these are your areas of expertise, as is your discipline knowledge. It should also be noted that you are not responsible for examination outcomes. Ultimately the decision about whether or not to engage belongs to the child – teachers can only facilitate those who choose to do so.

The Workload of a Newly Qualified Teacher: Thinking about Planning

The NPPTI report drew attention to workload as one of the most pressing concerns for newly qualified teachers. As mentioned above, there is a very considerable difference in teaching workload between initial teaching placement and the first professional year. Newly qualified teachers spoke of 'endless work', 'overpowering' workload, and the 'intensity' of the job (DES 2006:87). They found that most of their personal time was occupied in preparation, correction or simply 'thinking' about schoolwork. They also reported feeling that there was not enough time 'to cover the vast amount of material and required subject matter', that the workload precluded meaningful interaction with individual pupils and that 'preparation and correction(s) seem to take hours' (DES 2006:87). A striking outcome of this pressure was that newly qualified teachers found that they had little or no time to prepare formal lesson plans; an inherently essential part of good teaching.

Therefore, before beginning of term, study the teaching load allocated to you. Invariably, it will be significantly greater than the workload you encountered during teaching placement, will include examination classes and, possibly for the first time, exposure to senior groups. This requires significant preparation. You must plan the year ahead, taking account of breaks, holidays, examination periods and so on.

You must also be aware of the greater intensity demanded in teaching senior and examination groups. You must prepare a yearly plan of work for these, as you should do for all groups, but be aware of the need to include revision periods and space for oral and aural examinations. Do not underestimate the demands of teaching these groups, particularly at Leaving Certificate level. You must have mastery of your content area and be able to teach it in a fluid and accessible manner. You should try this at home, practising delivery and thinking about possible questions pupils may ask.

Be prepared for a challenging and tiring first few months, accept this as part and parcel of beginning teaching, don't fret that you are so tired in the evenings, make sure to get enough rest and pace your day and week. Importantly, be sure to make time for personal relaxation at some stage during the week and at weekends. If it helps, remember that this too will help you be a better teacher because you will be more refreshed, energised and detached.

Discipline: A Key Worry for Newly Qualified Teachers

As already discussed, discipline and behaviour are areas of concern for newly qualified teachers, but you should not feel alone in this regard. We saw above that newly qualified teachers ranked this, in terms of requiring support, second only to that of working with pupils with special needs. Newly qualified teachers working in designated disadvantaged schools encounter the greatest challenges and the NPPTI Report (page 88) notes that this group found 'the initial weeks and months of teaching very difficult and stressful', often leading them to express doubts about their career choice. You should not, therefore, be surprised to encounter challenges in this area. Look at Chapter 6 again and keep in mind that poor behaviour is very rarely directed at you personally, rather at your persona as teacher and representative of the school or wider adult society. While this does not mean that we are not angered, saddened or frustrated by poor behaviour, it should help to create a mental barrier between it and us, but not between the pupil and us. Remember the difference between the sin and the sinner!

It is also important to remember that you are not alone. Your more experienced colleagues will also be coping with poor behaviour and in numerous schools, newly qualified teachers will be facing challenging and stressful situations. However, the vast majority of teachers find that, gradually, problems associated with poor behaviour have a way of dissipating. We get to know the pupils better, we discover ways of working with this age group, we learn to take ourselves a little less seriously, we recognise that it is important to learn how to choose our battles, when to bend in the wind and when to stand firm.

As the first few years of teaching pass, we find that as pupils come to us in later years, we will have taught them when they were younger, they know us, how we operate and where the boundaries are. We cannot emphasise enough that classroom management is based upon sensible rules, building good relationships with pupils and being work-oriented. It requires invention and preparedness to try again, to reflect, to admit to mistakes and ultimately to believe that, in almost all cases, you will succeed.

Other Demands of the First Year of Teaching

Newly qualified teachers report that their first experience of professional teaching is stressful and tiring. Given that the supports of the teaching degree or diploma are now absent and that they are now fully immersed in a school, they also report feelings of isolation. These are very common experiences and tiredness is a particularly common complaint.

Student-teachers, who usually have a much lighter workload than NQTs, complain of extreme tiredness after teaching. While, in some part, this is because of anxiety around teaching, it is also the outcome of the teaching activity itself. Again, with time and the acquisition of a keener sense of pace, this becomes easier, but NQTs and student teachers, should be under no illusion about the physical and mental toll exacted by teaching. Those who join teaching from high-profile and (seemingly) more prestigious occupations constantly express surprise at how demanding and tiring teaching is. The NPPTI Report (page 89) recounts how NQTs experienced 'extreme tiredness and fatigue ... particularly during the first term'.

The demands on NQTs are considerable. One NQT reported that the work was so demanding that, by mid-term, 'I feel tired and may have already lost some of my enthusiasm', while another remarked that unless discipline improved in the school her teaching days were 'numbered', remarking that she was losing 'sleep and weight' (DES 2006:89).

It is important that NQTs share these feelings with colleagues, friends and family. Fatigue is an obstacle to healthy living and productive work. While a certain amount of tiredness is to be expected, the situation described by the last NQT is unfortunate and troubling. People have other responsibilities – family, children, a partner, husband or wife – but also themselves and their pupils.

Resist the temptation to commit to teaching in such a manner that you become preoccupied, that it takes time away from others who deserve or need your time. Newly qualified teachers should find ways to counteract stress and tiredness. Reflecting on the pace of lessons, the day and the week, finding time for activities and hobbies, sharing your concerns with friends, family or colleagues, seeking out relaxation techniques and always remembering that you can only do your best and that, ultimately, the decision to learn lies with your pupils and not with you, can all help to lend perspective and calm to a busy, stressful and demanding occupation.

Appendix

Supervision of Teaching Practice Placement: Guidelines and Suggestions

WHAT IS TEACHING PRACTICE SUPERVISION (TPS)?

All student teachers undergo some form of supervision during their teaching practice placement. As this varies between institutions, it is not possible to give specific guidelines regarding procedures. However, there are commonalities of approach and, as a general rule, supervision has similar objectives and expected outcomes.

TPS usually entails the classroom-based supervision/observation of the student-teacher by an expert. As a rule, the supervisor will arrive at an appropriate time before the beginning of the lesson, observe the entire period and spend some time in conversation with the student afterwards. Most institutions use an observation or evaluation form. The supervisor uses this to record the achievements and the areas for development that they have observed during the lesson and this usually forms the basis of the post-lesson feedback session.

WHAT IS THE PURPOSE OF TPS?

The purpose of supervision is twofold: evaluative and supportive. In other words, while, ultimately, the supervisor is responsible for deciding upon a grade that appropriately reflects the student-teacher's ability to teach (that is, to facilitate learning), s/he is also an important figure in the support mechanism offered by the teacher education institution. It is important that the student teacher recognises this and strives to enter into a collaborative working relationship with the supervisor.

New ideas, methods that worked well or failed, difficulties and successes should be shared with the supervisor. The student-teacher should seek advice whenever possible and, above all, demonstrate that s/he is able to reflect seriously upon what is happening in the classroom, leading to a preparedness to alter approaches, methodologies, customs, regulations and dispositions in order that learning might take place in an appropriate environment. Consequently, an engaged and committed student-teacher will eagerly anticipate the supervisory visit as an opportunity to test ideas, plan, ask questions, seek guidance and receive feedback.

WHAT IS EVALUATED IN TPS?

The precise elements of teaching practice evaluation differ between institutions. Each has its own method and procedure of observation and evaluation. Naturally, you should become familiar with the procedure operating in your institution as soon as possible. These may be provided in the course handbook or available from the administrator attached to your institution.

TPS requires the evaluation of multiple elements and it is not possible to provide an exhaustive list. Above all, supervisors are looking for the appropriate disposition: a student that is willing to learn, is committed, is willing to make changes, to try new methods, to reflect seriously on classroom practice and, most important, whose pupils are evidently learning. The student-teacher, therefore, has to plan well, teach well and be able to reflect on that teaching. Planning for each lesson is a fundamental requirement. Thoughtful planning, thorough preparation of content material, the use of resources (if appropriate), consideration of the requirements of mixed ability teaching, reflection upon the possible weakness in your plan and provision for a 'Plan B' are all prerequisites of sound classroom planning.

Of course, the plan is merely that; the actual classroom environment on a given day can readily make your plan seem redundant. However, at the heart of your classroom teaching is effective learning. This does not happen by accident and the supervisor will be attentive to ordinary good practice, such as classroom management, physical movement in the room, scanning, questioning, board work, independent learning, voice projection, appropriate level of instruction, use of praise and encouragement, movement between phases of the lesson, clarity of explanation and directions, timing, use of resources (including texts), disposition, professionalism, ability to 'think on your feet', variety of teaching approaches and methodologies, and a preparedness to seek imaginative ways of helping pupils to learn.

No two teachers teach in the same way. Two student-teachers using the same lesson plan will employ very different approaches, reflecting the influence of their personality and disposition towards teaching and pupils. Disposition, in other words your attitude towards teaching and learning, is important. Beautifully crafted lesson plans and state-of-the-art resources are of little use if the student-teacher is not wholly committed to helping his/her pupils learn. A commitment to learning is recognisable immediately; it is often revealed in the manner in which a teacher talks with pupils, seizes opportunities to engage them, asks questions, and encourages and challenges them. A genuine eagerness to see pupils learn, to engage them and to plan accordingly are some of the characteristics of good teaching. Many more are learned in the initial years of teaching, but supervisors are keen to see this commitment, founded on thorough planning coupled with the best possible efforts in the classroom.

Supervision also takes your professionalism into account. This includes your punctuality, dress, appearance, content knowledge, use of school procedures and general administrative apparatus. Teaching involves being part of the school community and your teaching practice supervisor will be anxious to know the extent to which this has taken place.

Therefore, if we were to offer three elements upon which teaching practice is evaluated these would be:

- Planning and preparation.
- Classroom teaching.
- Professionalism.

Student-teachers should be reassured that, ultimately, supervisors are looking for a willingness to learn and to improve. They are looking for potential, to see that you are developing your classroom practice along lines that will lead you to become an excellent teacher – you may not be there yet, but you will get there.

Recommended Reading

There is a very wide range of books available concerning the study of teaching. However, most of these are published in the UK and concentrate upon initial teacher education programmes in that country, which differ considerably from those pertaining in Ireland. The books listed below, however, contain valuable advice and information about the general challenges faced by student teachers and offer useful advice on all aspects of ITE.

Bennet, Hazel (2006) *The Trainee Teacher's Survival Guide*, Continuum, UK.

Butt, Graham (2003) *Lesson Planning*, Continuum, UK.

Capel, Susan *et al.* (2005) *Learning to Teach in the Secondary School: A Companion to School Experience*, Routledge, London.

Cohen, Louis, Manion, Lawrence and Morrison, Keith (2004) *A Guide To Teaching Practice*, 5th edn, Routledge, London.

Davies, Susan (2006) *The Essential Guide to Teaching*, Pearson Longman, UK.

Dixie, Gererd (2003) *Managing Your Classroom*, Continuum, UK.

Griffin, Sean and Shevlin, Michael (2007) *Responding to Special Educational Needs: An Irish Perspective*, Gill & Macmillan, Dublin.

Holmes, Elizabeth (2005) *Teacher Well Being*, Routledge Falmer, London.

Kahn, Peter and Walsh, Lorraine (2006) *Developing Your Teaching: Ideas, Insight and Action*, Routledge, London.

Kyriacou Chris (2007) *Essential Teaching Skills*, 3rd edn rev., Nelson Thorne, UK.

Marland, Michael (1993) *The Craft of the Classroom: A Survival Guide*, 2nd edn rev., Heinemann Educational Books, UK.

Roffey, Sue (2007) *The New Teacher's Survival Guide to Behaviour*, Paul Chapman Publishing, London.

Skinner, Don (2005) *Get Set for Teacher Training*, Edinburgh University Press Ltd, Edinburgh.

Watkins, Chris *et al.* (2007) *Effective Learning in Classrooms*, Paul Chapman Publishing, London.

Bibliography

Adler, A. (1930) *The Education of Children*, Gateway Publications, South Bend, Indiana.

Argyris, M. and Schön, D. (1974) *Theory in Practice. Increasing Professional Effectiveness*, Jossey-Bass, San Francisco.

Argyris, M and Schön, D. (1978) *Organizational Learning: A Theory of Action Perspective Reading*, Addison-Wesley Publishing Company, MA.

Ashcroft, K. and Foreman-Peck, L. (1994) *Managing Teaching and Learning in Further and Higher Education*, Falmer, London.

Atherton, J. S. (2005) *Learning and Teaching: Reflection and Reflective Practice* [Internet]. Available from: www.learningandteaching.info/learning/reflecti.htm.

Atherton, J. S. (2005) *Learning and Teaching: Critical Reflection* [Internet]. Available from: www.learningandteaching.info/learning/critical1.htm.

Baker, C. (2006) 'Enriching Teaching and Learning with AfL', *TL21 Newsletter Edition*, Number 4, Winter 2006/2007, pp.6–7.

Ball, M. Hughes, A. and McCormack, W. (2006) *Dyslexia: An Irish Perspective*, Blackhall Publishing, Dublin.

Barklay, R. A. (1997) *ADHD and the Nature of Self-Control*, Guildford Press, New York.

Beveridge, S. (1999) *Special Educational Needs in Schools* 2nd edn, Routledge, London.

Black, P., Harrison, C., Lee, C., Marshall, B. and Wiliam, D. (2003) *Assessment for Learning: Putting it into Practice*, Open University Press, Milton Keynes.

Black, P. and Wiliam, D. (1998) *Inside the Black Box: Raising Standards through Classroom Assessment*, King's College, London [Internet]. Available from: powayusd.sdcoe.k12.ca.us/projects/literacy/SSTTL/AssessDocs/PDFs/BlackBox_Article.pdf.

Black, P., Harrison, C., Lee, C., Marshall, B. and Wiliam, D. (2003) *Assessment for Learning: Putting it into Practice*, Open University Press, Milton Keynes.

Bloom, B. S. (1956) *Taxonomy of Educational Objectives, Handbook I: The Cognitive Domain*, David McKay Co. Inc., New York.

Booth, T. (1998) 'The poverty of special education: theories to the rescue?'

in: Clark, C., Dyson, A. and Millward, A. (eds) *Theorising Special Education*, Routledge, London, pp. 79–89.

Brookfield, S. (1995) *Becoming a Critically Reflective Teacher*, Jossey Bass, San Francisco.

Brookfield, S. (1998) 'Critically Reflective Practice', *Journal of Continuing Education in the Health Professions*, V. 18, No. 4, pp. 197–205.

Byers, R. and Rose, R. (1996) *Planning the Curriculum for Pupils with Special Educational Needs*, David Fulton, London.

Cooper, J. (ed.) (1999) *Classroom Teaching Skills*, Houghton Mifflin, Boston.

Cooper, J. (ed.) (2005) *Classroom Teaching Skills* (7th edn), Houghton Mifflin, Boston.

Cotton, K. (1988) *Classroom Questioning* [Internet]. Available from www.nwrel.org/scpd/sirs/3/cu5.html.

De Garmo, C. (1902) *Interest and Education: The Doctrine of Interest and its Concrete Application*, MacMillan, London. Available from: www.archive.org/stream/interesteducatio00degarich/interesteducatio00degarich_djvu.txt.

Department of Education and Science (2001) *Report of the Task Force on Autism: Educational Provision and Support for Persons with Autistic Spectrum Disorders*, Stationery Office, Dublin.

Department of Education and Science (2002) *Report of the Task Force on Dyslexia*, Stationery Office, Dublin.

Department of Education and Science (2006) *Report of the National Pilot Project on Teacher Induction*, Stationery Office, Dublin.

Department of Education and Science (England and Wales) (1978) *Report of the Committee of Inquiry into the Education of Handicapped Children and Young People*, HMSO, London.

Dewey, J. (1933) *How We Think: A Restatement of the Relation of Reflective Thinking to the Educative Process* (revised edn), D. C. Heath, Boston.

Donato, R. (2003) 'Action Research', *ERIC Digest* EDO-FL-03-08, December 2003.

Dreikurs, R. (1990) *Children: The Challenge*, Penguin Plume, New York.

Frederickson, N. and Cline, T. (2002) *Special Educational Needs, Inclusion and Diversity: A Textbook*, Open University Press, Milton Keynes.

Freire, P. (1970) *Pedagogy of the Oppressed*, Continuum, New York.

Gardner, H. (1983) *Frames of Mind: The Theory of Multiple Intelligences*, Basic, New York.

Garnett, J. (1994) *Differentiating the Secondary Curriculum: Marking Written Work*, Wiltshire Education Support & Training, Trowbridge.

Ginnis P. (2001) *The Teacher's Toolkit*, Crown House Publishing, Wales.

Hall, S. (1997) *Forms of Reflective Teaching Practice in Higher Education*, Teaching Learning Group [Internet]. Available from: lsn.curtin.edu.au/tlf/tlf1997/hall1.html.

Hall, T. (2002) *Differentiated Instruction*, National Center on Accessing the General Curriculum, Wakefield, MA [Internet]. Available from: www.cast.org/publications/ncac/ncac_diffinstruc.html.

Hamachek, D. (1999) 'Effective Teachers: What they do, how they do it and the importance of self-knowledge', in: Lipka, R. and Brinthaupt, T. *The Role of Self in Teacher Development*, State University of New York Press, Albany.

Hart, S. (1996) *Beyond Special Needs*, Paul Chapman Publishing, London.

Hogan, P., Brosnan, A., de Róiste, B., MacAlister, A., Malone, A., Quirke-Bolt, N. and Smith, G. (2007) *Learning Anew: Final Report of the Research and Development Project Teaching and Learning for the 21st Century, 2003–07*, Education Department NUI Maynooth [Internet]. Available from: www.nuim.ie/TL21.

Hopkins, D. (1993) *A Teacher's Guide to Classroom Research*, Open University Press, Milton Keynes.

Horgan, G. (2003) 'Educable: disabled young people in Northern Ireland challenge the education system' in: Shevlin, M. and Rose, R. (eds) *Encouraging Voices: Respecting the Insights of Young People who have been Marginalised*, National Disability Authority, Dublin, pp. 100–120.

Ireson, J. and Hallam, S. (2001) 'Alternative Ways of Grouping Pupils in School' in: *Ability Grouping in Education*, Sage, London.

Johnson, D. and Johnson, R. (1997) *Cooperative Learning – Two heads learn better than one* [Internet]. Available from: www.context.org/ICLIB/IC18/Johnson.htm.

Kemmis, S. and McTaggart, R. (1988) *The Action Research Planner*, Deakin University Press, Geelong.

Kenny, M., Mc Neela, E., Shevlin, M. and Daly, T. (2000) *Hidden Voices: Young People with Disabilities Speak about their Second Level Schooling*, South West Regional Authority, Cork.

Kenny, M., Mc Neela, E. and Shevlin, M. (2003) 'Living and learning: the school experiences of some young people with disabilities' in: Shevlin, M. and Rose, R. (eds) *Encouraging Voices: Respecting the Insights of Young People who have been Marginalised*, National Disability Authority, Dublin, pp. 138–158.

Killen, R. (1996) *Effective Teaching Strategies*, Social Science Press, Australia.

Larrivee, B. (2000) 'Transforming Teaching Practice: becoming the critically reflective practitioner', *Reflective Practice*, 1:3, pp. 293–307.

Learning and Teaching Scotland: Assessment is for Learning [Internet]. Available from: www.ltscotland.org.uk/assess/about/index.asp.

Leitch, R. and Day, C. (2000) 'Action research and reflective practice: towards a holistic view', *Educational Action Research*, 8:1, pp. 179–193.

Loughran, J. J. (2002) 'Effective Reflective Practice: In Search of Meaning in Learning about Teaching', *Journal of Teacher Education*, 53, 33, pp. 33–43.

Lyons, N., Hyland, A. and Ryan, N. (eds) (2002) *Advancing the Scholarship of Teaching and Learning through a Reflective Teaching Portfolio: The University College Cork Experience*, University College Cork, Cork.

Magee, B. (1982) *Popper*, Fontana Paperbacks, Glasgow.

Malone, G. and Smith, D. (1996) *Learning to Learn*, NASEN, Tamworth.

Marzano, R.J., Gaddy, B.B. and Dean, C. (2000) *What Works in Classroom Instruction?* [Internet]. Available from: www.mcrel.org/ topics/ Instruction/products/110.

McKeachie, J. Wilbert (1999) *Teaching Tips: Strategies, Research and Theory for College and University Teachers* 10th edn, Houghton Mifflin Company, Boston.

McMahon, Tim (1999) 'Is reflective practice synonymous with action research?', *Educational Action Research*, 7:1, pp. 163–169.

McNamara, S. and Moreton, G. (1995), *Changing Behaviour: Teaching Children with Emotional and Behavioural Difficulties in Primary and Secondary Schools*, David Fulton, London.

McNiff, J., Lomax, P., and Whitehead, J. (1996) *You and Your Action Research Project*, Routledge, London.

Mezirow J. (1991) *Transformative Dimensions of Adult Learning*, Jossey-Bass, San Francisco.

Moore, A. and Ash, A. (2002) 'Reflective practice in beginning teachers: helps, hindrances and the role of the critical other'. Paper presented at the Annual Conference of the British Educational Research Association, University of Exeter, England, 12–14 September 2002.

National Council for Curriculum and Assessment (2002) *Draft Guidelines for Teachers of Students with [Mild/Moderate/Severe and Profound] General Learning Disabilities*, The Authors, Dublin.

National Council for Curriculum and Assessment website, www.ncca.ie.

Nesbit, T., Leach, L., and Foley G. (2004) 'Teaching adults' in: Foley, G. (ed.) *Dimensions of Adult Learning: Adult Education and Training in a Global Era*, Allen & Unwin/Open University Press, London.

Nichols, S., Tippins, D. and Wieseman, K. (1997) 'A "Toolkit" for Developing Critically Reflective Science Teachers' Research' *Science Education*, 27(2), pp. 175–194.

Nolan, J. and Francis, P. (1992) 'Changing perspectives in curriculum and instruction' in Glickman, C. D. (ed.) *Supervision in Transition Yearbook of the Association for Supervision and Curriculum Development* (ED344277). Available from: http://eric.ed.gov/ERICWebPortal/ custom/portlets/recordDetails/detailmini.jsp?_nfpb=true&_&ERICExt Search_SearchValue_0=ED344277&ERICExtSearch_SearchType_0=no &accno=ED344277

O'Brien, T. and Guiney, D. (2001) *Differentiation in Teaching and Learning: Principles and Practice*, Continuum, UK.

Race, P. (2007) *The Lecturer's Toolkit: a practical guide to assessment, learning and teaching*, Routledge, London.

Rose R. and Howley M. (2006) *Special Educational Needs in Inclusive Primary Classrooms*, Paul Chapman Publishing, London.

Rotter, J. B. (1954) *Social Learning and Clinical Psychology*, Prentice-Hall, New York.

Schön, D. (1983) *The Reflective Practitioner: How Professionals Think in Action*, Basic Books, New York.

Schön, D. (1987, 1996) *Educating the Reflective Practitioner: Toward a New Design for Teaching and Learning in the Professions*, Jossey-Bass, San Francisco.

Schön, D. (1992) *The Reflective Turn: Case Studies in and on Educational Practice*, Teachers College Press, New York.

Shevlin, M. and Rose, R. (eds) (2003) *Encouraging Voices: Respecting the Insights of Young People who have been Marginalised*, National Disability Authority, Dublin.

Shulman, L. S. (1986) 'Those Who Understand: Knowledge Growth in Teaching, *Educational Researcher*, 15, 2, pp. 4–14.

Stiggins, R. J. (2002) 'Assessment crisis: the absence of assessment FOR learning', *Phi Delta Kappan*, 83 (10), pp. 758–765.

Swaffield, S. and Dudley, P. 'Assessment literacy for wise decisions'. A publication commissioned by the Association of Teachers and Lecturers National College for School Leadership Networked Learning Group.

Swain, J., French, S. and Cameron, C. (2003) *Controversial Issues in a Disabling Society*, Open University Press, Milton Keynes.

Vygotsky, L. (1986) *Thought and Language*, Massachusetts Institute of Technology, Cambridge, MA.

Watson, N., Shakespeare, T., Cunningham-Burley, S., Barnes, C., Corker, M., Davis, J. and Priestley, M. (1999) *Life as a Disabled Child: A Qualitative Study of Young People's Experiences and Perspectives*, Final Report, Economic and Social Research Council (ESRC) Research Programme.

Westwood, P. (1997) *Commonsense Methods for Children with Special Needs*, Routledge, London.

www.geoffpetty.com/activelearning.html.

Young, E. (2005) *Assessment for Learning: Embedding and Extending* [Internet]. Available from: www.ltscotland.org.uk/assess/for/index.asp.

Žižek, S. (2005) *The Parallax View*, MIT Press, Cambridge.

Index